CHARACTER AND COMEDY

BY THE SAME AUTHOR

UNIFORM WITH THIS VOLUME

OVER BEMERTON'S
LISTENER'S LURE
LONDON LAVENDER
MR. INGLESIDE
ROSE AND ROSE
GENEVRA'S MONEY
OLD LAMPS FOR NEW
FIRESIDE AND SUNSHINE
LOITERER'S HARVEST
ONE DAY AND ANOTHER
THE GENTLEST ART
EVENTS AND EMBROIDERIES
THE FRIENDLY TOWN
LUCK OF THE YEAR

CHARACTER AND COMEDY

BY

E. V. LUCAS

METHUEN & CO. LTD.
36 ESSEX STREET W.C.
LONDON

First Published	. . . . .	September	1907
Second Edition	. . . . .	October	1907
Third Edition	. . . . .	December	1907
Fourth Edition	. . . . .	November	1908
Fifth Edition	. . . . .	December	1909
Sixth Edition	. . . . .	October	1910
Seventh Edition	. . . . .	January	1915
Eighth Edition	. . . . .	December	1917
Ninth Edition	. . . .	September	1920
Tenth Edition	. . . .		1928

PRINTED IN GREAT BRITAIN

PREFATORY NOTE

THE Essays that make up this volume have been collected by permission from various periodicals. "My Cousin the Bookbinder" appeared in the *Cornhill Magazine*: the others in the *Outlook*, *T. P.'s Weekly*, the *County Gentleman*, and the *Academy*. In almost every case I have altered and expanded the text, I hope for the better. The second half of the book consists of a selection from an epistolary series that ran through *Punch*, which the proprietors kindly allow me to reprint here.

E. V. L.

CONTENTS

	PAGE
'MY COUSIN THE BOOKBINDER'.	1
A FUNERAL	14
MEDITATIONS AMONG THE CAGES	20
TWO IRISHMEN	29
FROM PERSIA TO ABERDEEN	45
THE SEARCH AND THE GIFT	57
A PHILOSOPHER THAT FAILED	63
A SKETCH BOOK	70
THE BEATING OF THE HOOFS	84
OUR GARDENERS AND LUCK OF THE WOODS	98
CONJURER AND CONFEDERATE	108
SISTER LUCIE VINKEN	116
LIFE'S LITTLE DIFFICULTIES—	
I. THE WEDDING PRESENT	125
II. JANE'S EIGHTH OR NINTH	133
III. THE CHAUFFEUR	141
IV. THE DEDICATION	149

LIFE'S LITTLE DIFFICULTIES (*continued*)—

    V. THE APPOINTMENT 157

    VI. THE TESTIMONIAL 164

    VII. THE BOX 172

    VIII. THE DOCTOR'S VISIT . . . 179

    IX. THE LOIN OF PORK 187

    X. THE SHADE OF BLUE . . . 197

    XI. THE SMITHSONS, THE PARKINSONS, AND
        COL. HOME-HOPKINS . . . 202

    XII. "WHITE PININGS" 210

    XIII. THE CHRISTMAS DECORATIONS . . 218

    XIV. THE PRIZE COMPETITION . . . 226

    XV. THE CRICKET CLUB CONCERT . . 233

CHARACTER & COMEDY

"My Cousin the Bookbinder"   *◦*   *◦*

"Oh, I am so poorly! I waked it at my cousin's, the bookbinder, who is now with God."—*Charles Lamb to P. G. Patmore*, 1827

"SO you've been reading that, sir, have you? I have a copy too. I'll fetch it and show you. . . . The inscription? Oh yes, that's all right. He's my cousin, true enough: his real name's not Elia, of course; his real name's Lamb—Charles Lamb. He's a clerk at the East India Company's in Leadenhall Street—a little dark man with a large head. Must be nearly fifty by this time.

"'Genius,' you say? Well, I've heard others say that too—one or two persons, that is: customers of mine; but I don't know. Perhaps I'm no judge of such things. I'm a bookbinder. The outside of books is my line, not the inside. Oh yes, I've read Elia's Essays—not all through, perhaps, but here and there. Quite enough to tell, anyway.

A   I

" He must have his Joke "

"'Genius,' you say? My idea of genius is **not** that. I like a straightforward thing. Did you ever read the *Elegy in a Country Churchyard,* by Thomas Gray? Now, there's genius. So beautifully it goes—never a trip in the tongue from beginning to end, and everything so clear a child could understand it, and yet it's literature too. My little girl used to say it. *Rasselas,* too—do you know that? The Happy Valley and all the rest of it. That's genius, I think. But not this twisted stuff going backwards and forwards and one never feeling quite sure how to take it. I like a plain man with a plain mind.

"It's just the same with my cousin when you meet him. You never know what he's at. He's so nice sometimes, all heart, and friendly—and then the next time I have a notion that everything he says means something else. He leads me on to talk—just as I am talking now to you, sir,—and he seems to agree with what I say so warmly ; and then all of a sudden I see that he's just making fun of me all the time. He must have his joke. He comes in here sometimes on his way from the office, and precious little he does there, I can tell you. Oh, they're an easy lot, those East India clerks.

"But with all his odd ways and that mischievous mouth of his, his heart's in the right place. Very different from his brother, who died a year or so back. He was nothing to boast of; but the airs that man used to put on! I remember his father well—a little brisk man, wonderfully like Garrick, full of jokes and bright, quick ways. He was really a scrivener, but he didn't do much of that in those days, having fallen into an easy place with old Mr. Salt, the Member of Parliament, and a great man in the law. This Mr. Salt lived in the Temple, and little John Lamb—that is your Elia's father—he was his servant: did everything for him and lived in clover; Mrs. Lamb, she cooked. Mr. Salt was the generous kind—sent the boys to school and all the rest of it. They had it all their own way till the old gentleman died, and then things went wrong one after the other. It's too sad to talk about. . . .

"Except that Mrs. Lamb and her husband's sister, Miss Sarah—'Aunt Hetty' they used to call her—never quite hit it off, it was as happy a family as you'd ask for. But there came terrible times. . . . It's too sad. Where was I?—Oh yes, so you see that Mr. John Lamb, Esquire, who died the other day, had little enough to boast of, but he walked about as if he owned the earth. He used to come in here now and then to give me an order, and he threw it to me as if it was a bone and I was a dog. Many's the time I had it on my tongue to remind him what his father was, but I kept it back. A word unsaid is still to say. He was at the South Sea House, near his brother in Leadenhall Street, but they didn't have much to say to each other. Mr. John, he was a big, blustering, happy man, while this little one who calls himself Elia is all for quietness and not being seen, and having his own thoughts and his own jokes. They hadn't much in common. . . .

" Besides, there was another thing. There's a sister, you must know, sir, a wonderful wise woman, but she's not always quite right in her head, poor dear ; and when it was a question of whether someone had to promise to be responsible for her, or she must go to an asylum for the rest of her life, her younger brother, the writer of that book there, under your arm, said he would ; and he gave up everything, and has kept her—it was thirty years ago very nearly—ever since. Well, it was thought in the family and by their friends that John, who was a grown man at the time and a bachelor, and beginning to be prosperous, ought to have done more than he did, and I think that sometimes he thought so too, although he was usually pretty well satisfied with himself. Anyway, he didn't go to see his brother and sister much, and when he did I've heard that there was often trouble, because he would have his own way and argufy until he lost his temper. I was told as how he once had a dispute with Mr. Hazlitt the writer over something to do with painting, and knocked him down. Just think of knocking a man down about a matter of paint! But there's some high-handed men that would quarrel over anything.

"Like his little brother, he tried writing too, but he couldn't do it. He wrote a little tract on kindness to animals, and brought it here to be bound in morocco. Not to give away, mind, but to keep. 'Author's Copy' I had to letter it. . . . 'Kindness to animals,' I nearly said to him; 'what about kindness to sisters?' But I didn't say it.

"The sister? Ah yes, she's the pick. She's a great woman, if ever there was one. I know her better than any of them, because when they were living near here, and her brother—your Mr. Lamb, the author — was at his office, I often looked in with a pork chop or some little thing like that. There's no jokes about her, no saying things that she doesn't mean, or anything like that. She's all gold, my cousin Mary is. She understands everything, too. I've taken lots of troubles to her—little difficulties about my

children, and what not—and she understands
directly, for all she's an old maid, and tells me
just what I want to know. She's the clever one.
She can write, too. I've got a little book of her
stories and some poetry for children—here they
are—I bound them myself: that's the best bind-
ing I can do—real russia, and hand tooling, every
bit of it. Did she write all of them? No, she
didn't write all, but she wrote the best. Her
brother Charles did something to each, but I
don't mind that. I think of them as her books—
Mary's. If only she had better health, she would
write much better than he does; but her poor
head. . . . Every year, you must know, she goes
out of her mind for a little while. Oh, it's too
sad. . . .

" Have they many friends? Oh yes, a good
many. Most of them are too clever for me; but
there are some old-fashioned ones too, that they
like for old sakes' sake. They're the best. One
or two of them are very good customers of mine.
There's Mr. Robinson, the barrister, he brings
me lots of books to mend, and I've had work for
Mr. Aders, too. But as for your Mr. Lamb,—
Elia,—never a stitch will he let you put into any
book, even if it's dropping to pieces. Why, he
won't even take the dealer's tickets off them.
He never thinks of the outside of a book, but

you should see him tearing the heart out of them
by the light of one candle. I'm told he knows
more about what books are worth reading than
anyone living. That's odd, isn't it, and his father
a little serving-man! Life's full of surprises.
They say he knows all about poetry, too, and
helped the great poets. There's Mr. Wordsworth,
why, he dedicated a book to my cousin,—I've got
it here, *The Waggoner*, a pretty book it is, too,—
and Mr. Coleridge, who wrote about the old sailor
man and the albatross, he let my cousin put some
little poems of his own into one of his books. It
turns one inside out when one thinks of this, and
then of the old days and his father powdering Mr.
Salt's wig. But I suppose everyone's father had
to work once. Still, it's funnier when one belongs
to the same family.

"Now I come to remember it, his father used
to write a little too—free and easy pieces for a
charitable society he belonged to, and so on. It's
odd how writing runs in a family. But there
won't be any more Lambs to write—John left no
children, only a stepdaughter, and Charles and
Mary are single. This is the end. Well . . .

"Yes, they've moved from London now.
They're living in Islington. They used to live
in the Temple, for years, and then they went to
Covent Garden, over a tinman's. Miss Lamb

liked that better than the Temple, but her brother
liked the Temple best. It gave her more to do,
poor dear, during the day, because her sitting-
room window looked over Bow Street, and she
could see all that was going on. I'm afraid
Islington is very dull after that. She could see
the two great theatres, too, and they both love the
play.

" He wrote a farce once. I went to see it.
Nearly twenty years ago, at the Lane, when
Elliston had it. We had orders for the pit, my
wife and I, and the house was full of clerks from
the South Sea House and the East India House.
But it wouldn't do. *Mr. H.* it was called, and
the whole joke was about the man's full name.
But it wouldn't do. No one really minds names,
and his wasn't so monstrously bad—only Hogsflesh
when all was said and done. All his friends did
what we could for it, and the gentlemen from
the great offices cheered and clapped, but the
Noes got it. I never heard such hissing. I
climbed up on the seat to see how poor Miss
Lamb and her brother were taking it,—they were
right in front, just by the orchestra,—and there
was he, hissing away louder than anyone. Think
of it, hissing his own play! It's one of the best
jokes I ever heard. But she, poor dear, she was
just crying.

" Mr. Dyer, the Writer "

"No, he never tried the stage again, not to my knowledge. But I always say it wasn't a bad little play. If he'd only have let his sister touch it up, it would have been all right. She would have told him that Hogsflesh wasn't a good enough joke. She knows. . . .

"I went up to Islington to see them only last week, but he was out. A nice little cottage, but very quiet for her. Nothing to see but the houses over the way, and the New River, and the boys fishing for sticklebacks all day long. The river's absolutely in front of the house : nothing between you and it. Have you ever heard of Mr. Dyer, the writer? An old man, nearly blind. Well, he was coming away from my cousin's one day last year, and he walked bang into the water before anyone could stop him. Plump in. It's a wonder he wasn't drowned. There was an account of it in the *London Magazine* for December; for my cousin's a terrible man to serve up his friends and have jokes against them. He writes about everything just as it happens. I'm always expecting he'll have me in one of his essays. In fact, to tell you a secret, sir, that's why I read them. But I don't think he's got me yet.

"Yes, Islington's very different from Covent Garden, and the Temple too; for though the

"She has her Thoughts"

Temple is quiet enough, you've only got to pop into Fleet Street to be in the thick of everything. When they lived there she used to like doing her shopping in Fetter Lane, because it was at the top of the lane that she used to go to school years and years ago. For she's getting to be an old woman, you know. Let me see, how old is she?—Why, let's see, when was Mary born? It must have been 1763; no, it was 1764. Why, she'll be sixty this year.

"What does she do all day? Well, she reads a great deal, stories for the most part. And she sews. She's very good with her needle. And then she has her thoughts. And at night they play cards. He gets back pretty soon, you know. Those East India gentlemen they don't do too much, I can tell you, and I'm told he's one of the laziest. Always either talking or writing letters, I hear. There's a good story of him down there. One of the superiors met him coming in at about half-past ten, and he said to him, sharp-like, 'Mr. Lamb,' he said, 'you come very late.' And what do you think my cousin said, the impudent little fellow? 'Yes,' he said, as cool as you like, 'yes,' he said, 'but see how early I go,' he said. I can't say it as he did, because he stammers and stutters and I'm no mimic: but the brass of it shut the gentleman

up. My cousin told me himself. He likes to
tell you his good things; but I can't understand
a lot of them. Everyone has a different idea of
what's funny. I'm with him, though, about old
Munden: I could laugh at him all night.

" I'm troubled about them up there, so far
from London and the theatres and the noise.
It's a mistake to give up so much all at once.
And they've given up their regular evenings, too,
when people came in to play cards and talk.
You can't ask busy folk to go to Islington.

" My cousin told me some bad news last week.
She says that your Mr. Lamb,—Elia,—although he
has such an easy time and a large salary, wants
to leave the East India House and do nothing. I
hope they won't let him. I know enough of life
and of him to see what a mistake it would be.
It was a mistake to go to Islington: it will be a
worse mistake to retire. He says he wants to
live in the country; but he doesn't really.
Authors don't know what they want. I always
say that every author ought to have a bookbinder to advise him.

" She knows it's all wrong, poor dear, but what
can she do? He worries so. She sees him all
miserable, and after she's said all she can against
his plans, she agrees with them. That's like good
women   When they see that what must be must

be, they do their best. But it is very sad. . . .
It's her I'm so sorry for. He's the kind of man
that ought to go to business every day.

"Well, sir, good-night to you. I hope I haven't
been tedious with all my talk.

"No, sir, not quite a genius ; but very clever, I
grant you."

P.S.—Of Lamb's cousin, the bookbinder (now
with God), to whom there are two or three
references in the *Letters*, nothing is really known,
save that he died in 1827, and Lamb "waked it" at
his funeral to some purpose. He may have been
(and it is my theory that he was) only a distant
cousin. But if he were a first cousin, he was probably
the son of that aunt of whom we have no information
save that she gave the little Charles Lamb the cake
which he gave to a beggar. It is known that John
Lamb had two sisters—Aunt Hetty, who was unmarried and lived with the Lambs for twenty years,
and one other. This may have been the bookbinder's mother. I assume this aunt to be distinct
from Aunt Hetty, because Lamb says that she gave
him the cake on a holiday, and he returned to school
by way of London Bridge. This would locate her

in Southwark, where the Lamb family never lived ;
but of course Aunt Hetty may have sojourned in
Southwark for a little, and her nephew may have
visited her there. I feel certain that when he
made London Bridge the scene of the adventure
with the beggar, he meant it : it was not over such
reminiscences that he mystified his readers. On
the other hand, the bookbinder—if we are to
entertain the first-cousin theory—may have been
a son of a brother or sister of Lamb's mother ; but
nothing is ever said of any such relations of hers.
Most probably, I think, the bookbinder was not a
first cousin, and belonged to an older generation.
In 1827 Lamb was fifty-two ; probably the bookbinder was seventy. I have chosen early 1824 as
the time of this conversation, because *Elia* was
just published.

A Funeral ✿ ✿ ✿ ✿ ✿

IT was in a Surrey churchyard on a grey, damp
afternoon—all very solitary and quiet, with
no alien spectators and only a very few mourners;
and no desolating sense of loss, although a very
true and kindly friend was passing from us. A
football match was in progress in a field adjoining
the churchyard, and I wondered, as I stood by
the grave, if, were I the schoolmaster, I would
stop the game just for the few minutes during
which a body was committed to the earth; and I
decided that I would not. In the midst of death
we are in life, just as in the midst of life we are
in death; it is all as it should be in this bizarre,
jostling world. And he whom we had come to
bury would have been the first to wish the boys
to go on with their sport.

He was an old scholar—not so very old, either
—whom I had known for some five years, and had
many a long walk with: a short and sturdy Irish

gentleman, with a large, genial grey head stored
with odd lore and the best literature; and the
heart of a child. I never knew a man of so transparent a character. He showed you all his
thoughts: as someone once said, his brain was
like a beehive under glass—you could watch all
its workings. And the honey in it! To walk
with him at any season of the year was to be
reminded or newly told of the best that the
English poets have said on all the phenomena of
wood and hedgerow, meadow and sky. He had
the more lyrical passages of Shakespeare at his
tongue's end, and all Wordsworth and Keats.
These were his favourites; but he had read everything that has the true rapturous note, and
had forgotten none of its spirit.

His life was divided between his books, his
friends, and long walks. A solitary man, he
worked at all hours without much method, and
probably courted his fatal illness in this way. To
his own name there is not much to show; but
such was his liberality that he was continually
helping others, and the fruits of his erudition are
widely scattered, and have gone to increase many
a comparative stranger's reputation. His own
magnum opus he left unfinished; he had worked
at it for years, until to his friends it had come to
be something of a joke. But though still shapeless,

it was a great feat, as the world, I hope, will one day know. If, however, this treasure does not reach the world, it will not be because its worth was insufficient, but because no one can be found to decipher the manuscript; for I may say incidentally that our old friend wrote the worst hand in London, and it was not an uncommon experience of his correspondents to carry his missives from one pair of eyes to another, seeking a clue; and I remember on one occasion two such inquirers meeting unexpectedly, and each simultaneously drawing a letter from his pocket and uttering the request that the other should put everything else on one side in order to solve the enigma.

Lack of method and a haphazard and unlimited generosity were not his only Irish qualities. He had a quick, chivalrous temper, too, and I remember the difficulty I once had in restraining him from leaping the counter of a small tobacconist's in Great Portland Street, to give the man a good dressing for an imagined rudeness—not to himself, but to me. And there is more than one 'bus conductor in London who has cause to remember this sturdy Quixotic passenger's championship of a poor woman to whom insufficient courtesy seemed to him to have been shown. Normally kindly and tolerant, his indignation on hearing of injustice was red hot. He burned at a story of meanness. It would haunt him all the evening. "Can ut really be true?" he would ask, and burst forth again into flame.

Abstemious himself in all things, save reading and writing and helping his friends and correspondents, he mixed excellent whisky punch, as he called it. He brought to this office all the concentration which he lacked in his literary labours. It was a ritual with him; nothing might be hurried or left undone, and the result, I might say, justified the means. His death reduces the number of such convivial alchemists to one only, and he is in Tasmania, and, so far as I am concerned, useless.

His avidity as a reader—his desire to master his subject—led to some charming eccentricities, as when, for a daily journey between Earl's Court Road and Addison Road stations, he would carry a heavy hand-bag filled with books, "to read in the train." This was no satire on the railway system, but pure zeal. He had indeed no satire in him; he spoke his mind and it was over.

It was a curious little company that assembled to do honour to this old kindly bachelor—the two or three relatives that he possessed, and eight of his literary friends, most of them of a good age, and for the most part men of intellect, and in one or two cases of world-wide reputation, and all a

little uncomfortable in unwonted formal black.
We were very grave and thoughtful, but it was
not exactly a sad funeral, for we knew that had
he lived longer—he was sixty-three—he would
certainly have been an invalid, which would have
irked his active, restless mind and body almost
unbearably; and we knew, also, that he had died
in his first real illness after a very happy life.
Since we knew this, and also that he was a
bachelor and almost alone, those of us who were
not his kin were not melted and unstrung by that
poignant sense of untimely loss and irreparable
removal that makes some funerals so tragic; but
death, however it come, is a mystery before
which one cannot stand unmoved and unregret-
ful; and I, for one, as I stood there, remembered
how easy it would have been oftener to have
ascended to his eyrie and lured him out into
Hertfordshire or his beloved Epping, or even
have dragged him away to dinner and whisky
punch; and I found myself meditating, too, as
the profoundly impressive service rolled on, how
melancholy it was that all that storied brain, with
its thousands of exquisite phrases and its perhaps
unrivalled knowledge of Shakespearean philology,
should have ceased to be. For such a cessation,
at any rate, say what one will of immortality, is
part of the sting of death, part of the victory of

the grave, which St. Paul denied with such magnificent irony.

And then we filed out into the churchyard, which is a new and very large one, although the church is old, and at a snail's pace, led by the clergyman, we crept along, a little black company, for, I suppose, nearly a quarter of a mile, under the cold grey sky. As I said, many of us were old, and most of us were indoor men, and I was amused to see how close to the head some of us held our hats—the merest barleycorn of interval being maintained for reverence' sake; whereas the sexton and the clergyman had slipped on those black velvet skull-caps which God, in His infinite mercy, either completely overlooks, or seeing, smiles at. And there our old friend was committed to the earth, amid the contending shouts of the football players, and then we all clapped our hats on our heads with firmness (as he would have wished us to do long before), and returned to the town to drink tea in an ancient hostelry, and exchange memories, quaint, and humorous, and touching, and beautiful, of the dead.

Meditations among the Cages ✧ ✧

DRIFTING somewhat aimlessly about the Zoo on Sunday afternoon, I came suddenly upon the hippopotamus's vast and homely countenance peering round the corner of its stockade. It is the hugest, most incredible thing—just for an instant a little like the late Herbert Campbell carried out to the highest power—and I felt for the moment as if I were in another world, a kind of impossible pantomime land. There was nothing frightening about it; it was more companionable than many faces that sit opposite one in a 'bus; and yet it was repellent, un-negotiable, absurd. It is not a thing to see suddenly.

This hippopotamus, who is now thirty years or more old, shows signs of age. Her feet are sore, her eyes are scaly, her teeth are few and awry and very brown. In bulk she is immense, of a rotund solidity unequalled in my experience. The Great Tun, filled with its gallons, would, one feels, be light compared with her. I could not help wondering what will happen when she dies, as die she must before very long : how her gigantic carcase will be moved, how dealt with, how eliminated. I am sure her lifeless form will be the heaviest thing in London—heavier than any girder, heavier than any gun. One has this impression, I suppose, because one knows something of the weight of an ordinary body, and one's mind multiplies that, whereas a girder or a gun conveys no distinct impression. Even the baby hippopotami, in the next cage, ridiculous little pigs of hippos, fresh from their packing-case and the voyage from Africa, are probably each heavier than four aldermen ; but the old one is fifty times heavier than the baby, and might easily, such is the consistency of her alarming barrel, be full of lead. When her tottering legs at length give way and she falls to rise no more, may I not be there to see !

Standing before this ridiculous mammoth, so useless and unwieldy, I failed utterly to understand the feelings of the big-game hunter who could deliberately shoot it. If ever there was an animal that should inculcate or encourage the maxim "Live and let live," it is the hippopotamus. I cannot understand how a man can dare to be responsible for adding so much

The best Short-slip

mortality to this already encumbered earth. And yet there are members of West End clubs sipping their coffee at this moment who have probably shot many. To kill a lion or tiger, or any of the active, dangerous beasts : I can understand that, although I wish never to do it; but to interrupt the already stagnant life of one of these gentle mountains—*that* I could never bring myself to do. How can one kill a creature that wallows ?

Falling in later with a zoological Fellow, with a head full of Greek and a pocket full of apples and onions, without which he never visits these friends, I learned many curious facts. Among other things, I learned that the hornbill, who looks a desperately fierce biped, prepared at a second's notice to stab one with his iron beak, even in the back, is really the kindliest and most companionable of birds, ready and eager for any amount of petting. He is also, perhaps, the best short-slip in the Gardens, for unwieldy as his beak looks to be, he can catch anything, throw it how you may. Albert Trott has hitherto been my ideal, but he reigns in my mind no more. *Le roi est mort ; vive l'hornbill.*

I cannot get over my surprise about the hornbill, whose favourite food, it ought to be known, is grapes. No animal looks much less tractable and nursable; yet as a matter of fact the horn-bill is as anxious to be noticed as a spoiled dog, and as full of sentimentality. Best of all—even more than grapes—he likes to be scratched under the chin, and he leans his head farther and farther back in the enjoyment of this ecstasy, until his bill points into the sky like the spire of a village church.

In close proximity to the hornbills live the boat-bill, who is as lovely as a Japanese print, and Pel's Owl, who has perhaps the richest eyes in the whole Zoo, and not the least melancholy life; for he, accustomed to fly lightly and noiselessly over the surface of African rivers, catching un-wary fish in his claws as he flies, is now confined to a cage within a cage, a few feet square. What must be his thoughts as he watches the sight-seers go by! What must be the thoughts of all these caged aliens! The seals and sea-lions, one can believe, are not unhappy; the otter is in his element; the birds in the large aviaries, the monkeys, the snakes—these, one feels, are not so badly off. But the beasts and birds of a higher spirit, a mounting ambition—the eagles and hawks and lions and tigers, and Pel's Owl—what a destiny! What a future! I would not think their thoughts.

I learned also from my instructive Fellow that

one of the llamas can expectorate with more precision and less warning than any American described by the old satirists; that the Bird of Paradise, exquisite and beautiful though he is, with every right to be disdainful and eremitic, will yet cling to the sides of the cage to eat a piece of apple from the hand, and, having taken it, swallow it whole; that the most westerly owl in the owl house will say "woof-woof" after anyone that it esteems; that eagles like having their heads stroked, and that there is one of them who, if you give it a lead, will crow like a cock. I doubt if such things should be. I like to think of the eagle as soaring into the face of the sun with an unwinking eye, and allowing no liberties. But in Regent's Park. . . . I suppose we must make allowances. Does not the rhinoceros eat biscuits?

I learned also that the thar loves orange-peel above all delicacies, and that the mountain goat who possesses the biggest horns can bring them down on the railings with a thwack that, if your finger chanced to be there, as it easily might, would assuredly cut it in two; but, on the other hand, that the slender, graceful deer in the pen near the elephants, who has lately lost one horn, is as gentle as a spaniel and greatly in need of sympathy.

In Delia's Arbour

I learned, also, that the baby elephant eats Quaker oats; and that there are keepers in the Gardens who have never yet seen the beaver, not because they keep looking the opposite way, but because that creature is so unaccountably shy. The only chance one has of catching a glimpse of him is at sunset.

But the introduction to Delia was the crown of the morning—the coping-stone of my good fortune in meeting this zoological friend. We spent an hour in her company, while she toyed with an assorted fruitarian dinner. I should not call her a slave to her palate: I never remember seeing a non-human animal (is she a non-human animal, I wonder?) so willing to drop a delicacy and turn to other things. She turned with chief interest to my walking-stick; but now and then the trapeze caught her restless eye, and she was on it; and now and then it seemed to be time to embrace or to be embraced. A very simple, loving soul, this Delia (is she a soul, has she a soul, I wonder?), with the prettiest little thumb imaginable — for an ourang-outang, and, so far as I could observe, no *arrières pensées*. Clean, too. In fact, quite one of us.

Delia is the first ape I ever saw that did not make me uneasy. So many monkeys—especially the larger apes—are such travesties of ourselves

The Diving Birds

—and not only such travesties, but now and
then such reminders of our worse selves—that
one regards them with an increased scepticism
as to man's part not only in this life, but in the
next. But Delia is winsome; Delia has the
virtues. She is kind, and gentle, and quiet. All
her movements are deliberate and well thought
out. She has none of the dreadful furtive sus-
piciousness of the smaller monkeys; so far as I
could see, no pettiness at all. And the hair that
serves her also for clothes, like Lady Godiva, is
a very beautiful rich auburn. I cherish her
memory.

It was the more pleasant to come under Delia's
fascination, because I had just seen that horrible
sight, the feeding of the diving birds. Here, at
the most, one said in Delia's warm basement-
room—here, at the most, is only mischief and
want of thought; here are no cruel predatory
jaws pursuing their living prey. The diving
birds give one, indeed, a new symbol for rapacity
and relentlessness, partly because the victims
which they catch with such accuracy and ferocity,
are so exquisitely made for joy and life. Can
there be anything more beautiful than a slender
diaphanous fish, gliding through the water with
the light of day inhabiting its fragile body? The
movements of a fish are in themselves grace in-

carnate. The keeper flings a dozen of these little miracles into the tank, and straightway they begin their magical progress through the green water. He then opens a cage, and a huge black and white bird, all cruel eye and snapping beak, plunges in, and in two minutes it has seized and swallowed every fish. The spectacle appeared to be very popular; but I came away sick.

I walked from Delia's boudoir to the lions, and from the lions to the sea-lions, by way of the long row of sheds where the nilghais and hartebeests and elands dwell, and found that the real interest of this house lay, not in those aliens, but in a domestic creature which, common though it be in English homes, is yet not too easy to observe—the mouse. If you want to see the mouse at ease, confidently moving hither and thither, and taking its meals with a mind secure from danger, go to the Zoo, nominally to study the eland. It is no injustice to the eland, who cares nothing for notice, therein differing completely from the male giraffe, who looks after his departing friends with a moist and wistful eye and a yearning extension of neck that only the stony-hearted can resist. The eland is less affectionate; he has no timidity, and he has no vanity. He does not mind what you look at, and therefore you may lavish all your attention on the mice that move about among his legs like the shadows of little racing clouds on a windy April day.

And so I came away, having seen everything in the Zoo except the most advertised animal of all—the pickpocket. To see so many visitors to the cages wearing a patronising air, and to hear their remarks of condescension or dislike, as animal after animal is passed under review, has a certain piquancy in the contiguity of this ever present notice, "Beware of Pickpockets," warning man against—what?—man. Lions, at any rate, one feels (desirable as it may be to capture their skins for hearthrugs), pick no pockets.

Two Irishmen ✎ ✎ ✎ ✎ ✎

THEY are King Bagenal and Edward Edge—
the autocrat and the gate-keeper. They
have nothing in common save their race and
their genuineness; but a book of essays, like misfortune, makes strange bedfellows.

Of King Bagenal I have discovered very little;
but it is all splendid. He was a king only by
the courtesy of the countryside, who knew the
royal stamp when they saw it; to the postman he
was Mr. Bagenal, of Dunleckny, in the county of
Carlow. But if ever regality coursed through a
wild Irishman's veins. . . You could not qualify
for the throne of a Bagenal merely by swagger
and bluster: you had to be what you professed to
be; you had to be a king right through. And
there is this to be said of the kings that get their
title from their neighbours—that they are kings
in fact, whereas a king in the more ordinary sense,
who comes to the title by descent, can very easily

be no king at all. His throne may be an accident, and he may never do more than sit nervously on the edge of it; but a King Bagenal leans back and lolls.

He was superb in his lawlessness and authority. Only two creators could have made King Bagenal. One is the God of Ireland; the other is George Meredith, who made Harry Richmond's Titanic father and the Great Mel.

This is how Daunt, in his *Ireland and her Agitators,* describes the monarch: "Of high Norman lineage, of manners elegant, fascinating, polished by extensive intercourse with the great world, of princely income and of boundless hospitality, Mr. Bagenal possessed all the qualities and attributes calculated to procure for him popularity with every class. A terrestrial paradise was Dunleckny for all lovers of good wine, good horses and dogs, and good society. . . . His politics were popular; he was the mover of the grant of £50,000 to Grattan in 1782. He was at that time member for the county Carlow.

"Enthroned at Dunleckny, he gathered around him a host of spirits congenial to his own. He had a tender affection for pistols; a brace of which implements, loaded, were often laid before him on the dinner-table. After dinner the claret was produced in an unbroached cask; Bagenal's

practice [his practice!] was to tap the cask with
a bullet from one of his pistols, whilst he kept
the other pistol *in terrorem* for any of his convives
who should fail in doing ample justice to the
wine.

" Nothing could be more impressive than the
bland, fatherly, affectionate air with which the
old gentleman used to impart to his junior guests
the results of his own experience, and the moral
lessons which should regulate their conduct
through life. ' In truth, my young friends, it
behoves a youth entering the world to make a
character for himself. Respect will only be
accorded to character. A young man must show
his proofs. I am not a quarrelsome person—I
never was—I hate your mere duellist; but experience of the world tells me that there are
knotty points of which the only solution is the
saw-handle. Rest upon your pistols, my boys!
Occasions will arise in which the use of them is
absolutely indispensable to character. A man, I
repeat, must show his proofs—in this world
courage will never be taken upon trust. I protest
to Heaven, my dear young friends, that I advise
you exactly as I should advise my own son.' And
having thus discharged his conscience, he would
look blandly round upon his guests with the most
patriarchal air imaginable."

"Heaven's Will be Done!"

"His practice," says Daunt, "accorded with his precept. Some pigs, the property of a gentleman who had recently settled near Dunleckny, strayed into an enclosure of King Bagenal's, and rooted up a flower-knot." The incensed monarch paved the way carefully to a challenge. "Nor was he disappointed. The challenge was given by the owner of the pigs; Bagenal accepted it with alacrity, only stipulating that as he was old and feeble, being then in his seventy-ninth year, he should fight sitting in his arm-chair; and that, as his infirmities preventing early rising, the meeting should take place in the afternoon. 'Time was,' said the old man with a sigh, 'that I would have risen before daybreak to fight at sunrise — but we cannot do these things at seventy-eight. Well, Heaven's will be done!'

"They fought at twelve paces. Bagenal wounded his antagonist severely; the arm of the chair in which he sat was shattered, but he escaped unhurt; and he ended the day with a glorious carouse, tapping the claret, we may presume, as usual, by firing a pistol at the cask."

There you have King Bagenal. This was little more than a hundred years ago. And to-day? What happens to-day when pigs trespass? An exchange of shots? Never. An exchange of lawyers' letters. How could his proud spirit

have brooked such meanness, such postponements!
Yes, it was well that he had to lay aside his
crown when he did. Life was rapidly becoming
too much for him. The whole course of events
was tending to squeeze out old gentlemen with
impulsive pistols; to-day there cannot be one left.
It is impossible to think of anything more incon-
gruous than King Bagenal in a police-station;
but had he lived to our monotonous time he
would of a certainty be often there, only at last
to be transferred permanently to a real prison to
await execution. How could he escape, and yet
how monstrous it would be!

King Bagenal died at the right time: before
duellists became murderers; before Father
Mathew set a fashion against carousals; before
every editor was a judge and jury. There is no
longer any premium on eccentricity. People
are terrified by it, and journalists, taking their
ideas from their readers, foster the fear. Dull-
heads, as Tennyson nearly said, are more than
"characters," and sheep-like faith than Irish
blood. Exeunt the royal race of Bagenals
Enter——

In spite of generations of reckless, combative
Irish gentlemen, it is odd that we have still to go
to American literature for the classical instances
of impetuosity with firearms. This is a reproach

to Irish authors which should touch them closely.
Irish gentlemen were killing and wounding each
other on sight almost for centuries before America
was heard of, and yet it was left for Bret Harte
and Mark Twain and John Hay in the Far West
to fix the type of fire-eater that carried his
honour in his belt. Perhaps a line or two from
the elegiacs on Thompson of Angel's will best
describe what I mean:—

"Light and free was the touch of Thompson upon his
    revolver,
Great the mortality incident on that lightness and freedom.

Why [Thompson is musing], why in my daily walks does
    the surgeon drop his left eyelid,
The undertaker smile, and the sculptor of gravestones
    and marble
Lean on his chisel and gaze? I care not o'er much for
    attention:
Simple am I in my ways, save but for this lightness and
    freedom."

Why were not similar elegiacs written years
before on Bagenal of Dunleckny? What is
wrong with Irish authors? But I would except
Lever, who, as a matter of fact, has Bagenal
himself in his *Knight of Gwynne*—or the scenario
of him—under the name of Bagenal Daly. Yet
how far from life!

To read of Bagenal and his contemporaries is

The Decay of Duelling

to be filled with wonder that any gentleman was left alive in Ireland at all. It was a state of society which at this day one simply cannot begin to understand. There are, Heaven knows, still enough ways of dying; but the short-tempered and accurate-shooting Hibernian is no longer one of them. Whether or not we are less courageous I do not know; but there is less engaging insolence about than there used to be, and less of conscious superiority. Jack not only was not as good as his master in King Bagenal's day, but he never thought he was. Similarly, his master then had no doubts; but to-day very few of us are quite certain about anything, either on earth or elsewhere. Duelling goes out very quickly when dubiety comes in. The duellist is one who is sure of himself and his ground. Mr. Bagenal had no doubts.

One word more of the Carlow King. The traditions of Dunleckny allege, says Daunt, that when Bagenal, " in the course of his tour through Europe, visited the petty Court of Mecklenburg-Strelitz, the Grand Duke, charmed with his magnificence and the reputation of his wealth, made him an offer of the hand of the fair Charlotte, who, being politely rejected by King Bagenal, was afterwards accepted by King George III." That sets the seal on his native royalty. The

King of England had to marry the King of Carlow's leavings. It was well for our satirical literature that Bagenal was firm, for where would Peter Pindar have been had Farmer George not married the Princess Charlotte? She was his best Muse.

And so we leave the uncrowned king and come to the gate-keeper.

All that I know of Edward Edge comes from a slender square book printed in 1899 in Alassio. It is compiled by H. H. W., and is entitled *Edgiana: Being a Collection of Some of the Sayings of Edward Edge*. Money cannot buy this book, which is as rare as an Elzevir, and much more humanly interesting.

It would be amusing to accumulate conjectures as to who and what this Edward Edge was. How long would it be, I wonder, before anyone guessed that he was the keeper of the gate at St. Patrick's Deanery in Dublin—Swift's own deanery, but in a later day, 1865 until the late eighties, when he was pensioned off, to die, aged about eighty, in 1894. That was Edward Edge's sphere of activity, and he adorned it, if not by any great distinction as a porter, at any rate with his flowers of speech. For Edge's niche in the Temple of Fame he owes to his tongue—to the readiness and freedom of it, to his store of odd epithets and sudden searching criticisms, and perhaps most of all to his vivid, although innocent, oaths. For just, as the French say, there is no need for a sculptor to be himself made of marble, so can a man keep a deanery gate and be no dean. Loyalty and fidelity Edge had to a degree not much, if any, less than a Christian martyr; but he did not allow the contiguity of St. Patrick's to chasten his nimble objurgatory fancy or modify his memories. Glory be! And H. H. W., in his turn, has not allowed the fear of wounding tender susceptibilities to stand in the way of a faithful reproduction of the old man's eloquence. You can, in fact, do a good deal in a book when you print it privately at Alassio.

The two richest Irish talkers of recent times are, I suppose, Terence Mulvaney and Martin Dooley. But both are imaginary: projections of men of genius. Edward Edge lived; his photograph is before me, a good deal like Charles Kingsley. Twenty years ago, the treasures of his vocabulary and the riches of his memory were at the service of anyone clever enough to get round him. And many a Dublin resident must remember him well. To draw Edge out, to lure him on to obiter dicta, became, indeed, a recognised pastime among the Dean's friends who were humorists, and it is eminently one of these who put together this very curious and perhaps unique little book.

Edge came from Wicklow, where he was born about the year of Waterloo, and where he spent the first fifty years of his life. Here is his genealogy :—

" Misther H., did ye ever hear tell of Edgware Road, in or about the city o' London? Well, th' Edges owned that, and bedambut I'm thinkin' the weighty part o' the county o' Middlesex. It was Isaiah Edge that come over wid William, and was at the siege o' Derry. There's some o' th' Edges wouldn't look at me now. There's ould Ben Edge, a cousin o' mine, that owns all the coal-mines in the Queen's County. There's a third cousin o' mine—John Edge—that's Sittin' Justice of Inja. The Queen come up to him in the sthreet in London, and she taps him on the shouldher, and she says, ' Begod I'll make ye Sittin' Justice of Inja,' and that's what he is this minute. Now I might be dyin' be the roadside, and fire the bit he'd offer furta stan' me the price of a pint !

" My sixth grandmother was a Jewganawt [Huguenot]. Faith, she had to gother together all her ould pooks an' wallets an' away wid her out o' the city o' Paris in the year 1572. My great-grand-mother knew Latin an' Hay-ber-doo [Hebrew], and bedambut she had the weighty part o' the Gurdeek [Greek] toongue. There's an

ould sesther o' mine, that's a terrible savin'
woman ; that wan id live on the clippins o' tin !
Faith, she'd go furder on a ha'penny nor I would
on two shillin' !

"Now isn't it a wondherful thing furta say, in
the regyard o' the breed o' th' Edges, that no
matther some o' them might 'a become poor brutes
and divils, there was never wan o' the breed that
turdned Roman ! "

He was a staunch Protestant, and loved to
attend controversial meetings at which Roman
Catholics were corrected and repudiated. That,
says his biographer, was probably all the religion
he knew—the glow of satisfaction upon the rout,
real or imagined, of the heretics. His hostility
to Rome was continual, as, indeed, became a good
" Dane's Man." Observe him before a portrait of
Cardinal Newman :—

"Sure, what the blazes does Misther John have
the likes of him on the wall for ? Heth an' if I
had that ould fella's picture, I'd fire him out on
the sthreet, and bedambut I'd *lep* on him, so I
would. [Going up close to the picture and
peering into it.] Musha, *a dam ould Roman eye ;
that's* what he has ! "

But he could be fair, too. " My opinion," he
said once, "it don't matter Adam what bl—y
denomination a man id belong ta ! Sure there's
rogues Roman an' there's rogues Prodesan' ! "

Pronunciation's Artful Aid

The old man could write and read with much difficulty ; hence probably the quaintness and personal character of his vocabulary, which—like a child's—consisted largely of words as he thought he heard them. Hence " alcohol" became " alcordn " ; " Protestant," " Prodesan " ; " Admiral," " Admirdle " ; " girl," " g'yairdle " ; "foreigners," "fawrdners " ; " colonel," "curdlan," and so forth. One book he had of which he never tired. *Culpeper's Herbal* — " The Culpeper " he called it—and drew all his remedies, save a few into which a modern spirit entered, from its depths.

Himself the soul of honesty, he delighted artistically in bold rogues, whatever their denomination might be; but probably preferred them, when bold, to be " Prodesan " — such as Frank Splay, the window-cleaner :—

" Well, ould Splay (the Catholic I call him, an' he all the time a good Prodesan) come into the lodge th' other night, about the time he was afther takin' Lord Plunket's pledge. ' Well, Frank,' says I, ' how didja fare yistherda' ? ' ' Aw, very well,' says he ; ' I was clanin' the windas for such and such an ould wan.' ' Tell me,' says I, ' and did she give ye a tundherin' fine dinner ? ' ' Faith, she did ; I eat may be 3 lbs. o' beef—the dinner was out o' the way good.' ' And did she give ye ne'er a hap'orth to dhrink ? ' ' Begob and

she did so ; " heth an," says she, " me poor man, I
believe your dinner isn't complate without the
dhrink ! " ' ' Begor I believe not, ma'am,' says he.
Well, what the divil should he do but he takes
and dhrinks two or three pints o' Guinness's finest.
' Aw, gog's bloog an' 'ounds,' says I to him, ' y'ould
thief Frank, but yer afther breakin' Lord Plunket's
pledge ! '

" ' Heth an' I am not,' says he ; ' sure I didn't
pay for the po-ert-ther ! '

" Aw, Frank's a great ould rogue entirely !

" Well, there was another time he was clanin'
for an ould lady on the Sarc'lar Road.   Mindja
there was an ould cupboard in the cordner wid
the divil a less nor a mather o' 3 lbs. o' beef in it.
Well, when th' ould wan had her back turdned
an' she out o' the room, what the blazes divilment
should he be up ta but he goes up to the cupboard
and bl—y end to the thruppence but he eat
every dambit o' the beef out o' that, and bad
luck t'all but he sticks the th' ould cat locked up
inside the cupboard.   Presently she comes down
to the kitchen an' opens the press.

" ' Aw, gog's bloog an' fury,' says she, ' the
cat's afther atin' all me beef on me I had for yer
dinner.   I'm sorry, me poor man, I've nothin'
furta give ye t'ate ! '   ' Faith, so am I, ma'am,'
says he, ' more's the pity ! '—an' he wid the 3 lbs.
o' beef in his ould body all the time, the great
ould thief.   Faith, Frank's a terrible cute chap
entirely in the regyard of all soorts o' divilment ! "

I quote a few of his detached sayings or *pensées*.

Various Obiter Dicta

Of the waves at Newcastle :—

" Aw ! the waves up here does be nothin' to-
wardst what there was below in Newcastle comin'
up to forty or fifty year ago.   There'd be waves
there, and bloog an' 'ounds there'd be room for
a whole regiment to march in undher the curdle
o' the wave wid th' arch it did make."

Of ablutions and shaving :—

" Sathurda' nights or Sunda' morn'ns is times
enough for a man to wash his hands ! sure a man
that id wash his hands more nor that, id have no
industhry ! "   [? Any etymological connection in his
mind with " Dust " ?]
" It's of a Sathurda' night I'd always tear the
heavy scoom off o' me puss wid th' ould razor."

Of a cure for a cold :—

" If it was a thing ye had a heavy surfeit o'
cowld, faith there's nothing betther ye could do
only take an' ate a rale terrible ould salty book
haird'n [buck herring !] that id give ye the divil's
drooth [drought, *i.e.* thirst], an' then nothin' id
sadisfy ye but ye *should* swally two or three
bookets o' cowld spring wather, an' agin yid be
in bed, be the tundherin' Mack, the lather o'
pesperation yid be in id sweep the cowld to blazes
out o' your body ! "

Concerning homœopathy :—

" Aw sure I know all about the Home-potticks ;
sure it was a woman in the city o' Paris that in-

Three Proud Boasts

vented it. Little seeds and ground airubs [herbs]
—that's the way the' goes to work!"

Of one who had been dismissed for drinking :—

"Well now, it's a quare thing furta say ould
XYZ should 'a been put out of it for the dhrink,
an' he as daycent a man as ever carried a shillin'!
Heth an' I always thought he was a man that
could *hould a sup without lettin' in !*"

Of a sportsman :—

"One o' the brothers was a docthor; th' other
follied shootin'—he'd be always shootin'—an'
gog's great tare an 'ounds but he was a *grand*
shot! All nations id be comin' furta shoot agin
him, but the' might as well 'a stopped at home.
Aw, there's nothin' that flies — nothin' undher
the stars—but he'd hit."

And here are three of his proud boasts :—

"There's not a man in all Ireland, put England
to it that same, that id be able furta hould a
candle to me in the matther o' puttin' down
doong!
"There's not a man in Ireland that id be able
to read the names over the shop-doors agin me!
"Misther H., I might be blind dhroonk, and
dammyskin I'd be safer in the regyard o' lockin'
and boultn' th' ould gate nor another man id be
an' he *black* sober !'"

Let me close with H. H. W.'s description of

this simple profane old man in all the glory of authority on a Sunday afternoon :—

"Punctually at 4.30 he would take his stand just outside the door, on the pavement, leaving the door ajar, to wait for the Dean's coming in from the Cathedral. Edge would often have more than half an hour to wait before the Dean appeared, but these were perhaps the proudest moments of the week for him, for in the meantime the departing congregation, including the *élite* of Dublin residents and visitors, some driving, some on foot, would have filed by ; and as he stood there, *endimanché* with clean collar and the best 'rig' he could muster, in full view of all 'the Quality' did they but turn their heads to see him, he experienced to the full a dignified consciousness of being 'the Dane's port-ther,' and moreover of executing that function 'betther nor any man in Ireland.'"

Edward Edges there must always be—transparent, humorous souls who do their duty and worship their masters—but with the spread of education and papers their speech is bound to become less individual and racy. The more praise, then, to H. H. W. for preserving for us these jewels that fell from the old gate-keeper's lips.

From Persia to Aberdeen ✑ ✑ ✑

IT is my misfortune to be just too late for most of the more dramatic incidents of the open air. Once, for example, walking with a naturalist in St. Leonard's Forest and lagging for some minutes behind him (the only time I had done so during the day), I joined him just as he was standing as still as a stone watching a bank. " If you had come a minute sooner," he said, " you would have seen a snake swallow her young." That is the kind of thing that happens to me.

Again, last year, I went to stay in a house under the South Downs close to a little spinney, and was met by the news that an old vixen had cubs there and everyone had seen them playing together. I need hardly say that I did not. Yet a lady that I know well, who cares nothing for these things, once came on a small fox-cub that had lost itself near Willingdon, in Sussex, and nursed it in her arms. I, who would value such

A Cat carrying Kittens

an experience rightly, will go down to my grave
and never find anything. Even moles elude me.

With the exciting untoward incidents of
civilised life I am equally unlucky. Last year,
for example, while at Cowes, on two distinct days
I followed a race for some hours, and left each, as
it turned out afterwards, only a minute or so
before the mast of one of the yachts was carried
away. I am not lucky. The harvest of my quiet
eye comprises little that is unusual. Horses have
always risen again before I can reach the crowd.
Fires are out. Men in fits have recovered.

But there is an exception now and then; and
I have seen a pretty thing to-day of which I had
before only heard and had much wanted to see.
I have seen a cat carrying her kittens.

This cat is even more unsatisfactory than the
generality of her selfish kind. Her life is more
resolutely detached from that of her owners; her
return for any kindness that is shown her is even
less spontaneous and noticeable. It is testimony
to the amazing cleverness of cats that they are
kept and fed at all, to say nothing of being petted.
It all comes back to the old truth that if you
want people to honour you, you must despise
them.

This cat began her career of tyranny by making
us walk five miles instead of two at the end of a

tiring day; but a houseful of beautiful wild creatures, blue and elusive as wood smoke, was compensation enough. Mélisande (as we will call her here) was one of them, and her second act of tyranny was to make us pay far too much for her, or, at any rate, more than I could afford. Her third was to catch an expensive cold, her fourth to have an expensive consort, and her fifth to have four expensive and delicate children. What their delicacy cost I have no notion, but there is a firm of veterinary surgeons whose books could tell.

For these kittens, I may remark, Mélisande cared nothing, and it is no exaggeration to say that her first display of anything like affection for her mistress coincided with the departure of the last of her family, bound for a neighbouring chemist, who puts an end to unfortunate animals at a shilling a head. Nothing in life, indeed, so became these kittens as their departure from it, for none of their medicaments to keep them alive had cost so little as this extremely reasonable *coup-de-grâce*.

We were soon to discover, however, that Mélisande's callous treatment of her first children resulted less from the want of maternal feeling than from a deep-rooted and almost passionate Radicalism that led her to desire by any means to debase

47

her blood and to despise everything that was of equally high lineage. For her long pedigree now reposing in my desk (which goes back even to Darius) she cared less than nothing. She believed in the people and was prepared to back her belief—even to consorting day and night with a perfectly awful sandy cat with a permanent black smudge on his left cheek. And now she has three new kittens—one jet black, one rather like herself but sadly democratised, and one tabby— and she loves them to distraction. It was these that I met her carrying, having decided to change her home from the wood stack to some more convenient address, nearer the kitchen.

On the strength of our experience with Mélisande, my advice would be—not to buy a pure-bred cat of great distinction. I am perhaps underrating the æsthetic pleasure which a Blue Persian can give. This I know can be intense, and there are moments when Mélisande is distractingly lovely—as lovely as a pearl-grey sea, or an evening mist. Her eyes, too, are of a burning orange unlike anything else in Nature. But although she is superlatively distinguished in her beauty, it must be remembered that there never was a cat that could do anything ugly. Even that vile sandy cat with the smudge to whom Mélisande gave her heart has the most exquisite

The best Cat I know

contours. The curves and graces of the ordinary household cat are perhaps for all practical purposes beauty enough for a working English home; and when to these is allied a dependent, or even proprietary, interest in the human members of the family—a dallying to be scratched, a purring on the hearth, and a coaxing presence at meals in the hope of a scrap—why, then, to anyone who values friendliness as I do, the ordinary cat becomes more to be desired than any prize-winning queen.

The best cat I know at this moment lives in Northamptonshire, and follows its master and mistress wherever they go, about the garden and fields—just like a dog, only with more circumspection. Whenever they stop the cat stops too, and perhaps leans against their legs. When they go on the cat goes on too, just behind, silently, composedly, like a shadow with a waving tail. I should like a cat that would do that. Instead, we have the costly Mélisande, who would not lift a finger if she saw me drowning.

I am only just beginning really to understand the nature of the Aberdeen. Our last was a very ingratiating little bitch, full of affection and roguishness, who, however, was with us for so short a time, and during that time was so occupied in thoughts as to how to evade our vigilance and be getting on with the true business of life, becoming a mother—that we never had the undress material workings of her mind at all. Even when most coquettish and endearing, even when putting in motion all the machinery of lovableness, with her head on one's chest and the ridiculous boot buttons which she called her eyes looking up into one's face, her brain, to a keen observer, was manifestly busy over one matter only, and that the old topic.

Precautions we had to take, because there were two very sound reasons why Betty ought not to have puppies yet. One was that she was far too young, being herself but a mere chit; and the other that the neighbourhood contained no husband of equal birth. But one might as well attempt to stop the tide as control these affairs. A male Aberdeen mysteriously appeared within call, and Betty's face assumed an expression of amused satisfaction. . . .

Her owners, however, who became wise only long after the event, had no suspicion. . . .

One day she disappeared, and was absent for so long—nearly a week—that we gave her up completely. And then one evening she suddenly was in the room again, very thin, very demonstrative, but also very nervous and restless. She ran to the door and back again. She whined all the time.

A Lesson Learnt

There is a story in a book that I read far too many years ago, when I was at my first school, which tells how a merchant who was travelling with a large bag of money sat down by the roadside to rest, and on resuming his journey forgot (as merchants do in stories, but nowhere else) his property. His dog, however, perceived the error, and, by jumping up at him and barking, did its best to impede his steps, make him think, and drive him back. The merchant endured this for some time, and then, persuaded that the creature was mad, and having tested it with water, which it was too unhappy to stop and drink, drew his pistol and shot it. The poor thing, bleeding horribly, crawled away and disappeared. Some hours afterwards the merchant at last missed his bag, hurriedly retraced his steps to his resting-place, and there found it safe and sound—with his dog's lifeless body stretched across it. True or untrue, this story made a great impression on me, and I remember determining never to be so foolish as to disregard, in the unimaginative mercantile manner, the dumb gestures of any animal; and therefore, when Betty had run to the door and back several times, I lit a lantern, tied a long string to her collar, and expressed my intention of going with her wherever she might lead, no matter how far.

Betty's Secret

She took me painfully at my word, dragging me at a gallop down an almost vertical bank, thick with brambles and very wet with dew. On and on I went, slipping and sliding and torn, until she suddenly disappeared as thoroughly as if the earth had swallowed her. As it indeed had, for she had entered a large deep hole under the roots of a tree. With great difficulty I hauled her forth again and stretched my arm into the hole as far as it would go, but could feel nothing. Meanwhile Betty was so pulling at the cord and fighting to get back again that I allowed her to do so, listening the while very attentively, and I was presently aware of a faint whimpering in the remoter recesses of this planet, and knew the secret of her absence and her retreat. She had puppies, and in her pride of motherhood had chosen to make her own home for them. No one should help. It was only because hunger had conquered that she had returned to the house.

Her pride, however, was not stubborn, and when the puppies were extricated with a rake and placed comfortably in a basket near the fire, she was the happiest mother that the Granite City ever sent forth.

With Betty my acquaintance with Aberdeens for a while ceased, for she soon after left us, and her one puppy that we kept early developed fits and died—the effect, I imagine, of his mother's maternal precocity. But recently I have taken up my studies in Aberdeen terrierdom again, having acquired direct from Aberdeen one Boby, who is, I am told, a fine example of the breed. He travelled alone at the age of four months from Scotland to St. Pancras, and was to be fetched in the forenoon. It was, however, later before that could be, and in the meantime he had thrown the Aberdeen spell over most of the parcels' office staff, and was surrounded by the luxuries of the season. I doubt if any other dog could do this as an Aberdeen can. It is a regular habit with them to have all they want. I have a theory that this is partly because they are so like little pigs. Everyone adores little pigs, and everyone would like to pet one; but nobody has ever done so. In default the Aberdeen puppy, who is the next thing to a little pig, receives a double share of attention—part for his likeness for that other and part for himself. His nose, too, must have a share in his victories. It is the thin end of the wedge made visible. The rest cannot but follow.

I don't know how it is with Aberdeens whom time has sobered into grisly fidelity, such as I see following their masters as dinghys follow yachts; but at the age of six months, judging by this Boby, they are not readily obedient, not brave, and not unselfishly affectionate. Such love as Boby offers is cupboard love purely. He adds to these defects a curious lack of enterprise: he cares nothing for a walk. If by any chance it is necessary to chastise him or even reprimand him when he is out—principally for eating unsuitable things—he runs straight home again, and, carrying his wounded heart into the kitchen (where he reigns), is healed in the usual manner. It is my experience that dogs do not vary much: each is a type of his breed; and so I make bold to deduce from Boby the generalisation that all Aberdeens are self-protective. Perhaps they get it from their country.

In a dog self-protectiveness is rather a grave defect, showing very black against the radiant whiteness of the character of the other dog here —a spaniel—who does all that one wants a dog to do: is very loyal, full of trust in you, brave, enterprising, and so much attached to his people that probably no amount even of actual cruelty would alienate him or cause him to prefer his own company. Indeed, he hates his own company; and that, I take it, is a virtue in a dog. But he has no finesse, no moods, no arts. You must take a spaniel for what he is—always the same. It is the special privilege of the

The Art of Begging

Aberdeen puppy to have temperament and wiles : to get back by stealth, by cleverness, by sheer force of personality and a capriciousness as well ordered as that of any pretty actress, all and more that he may be in danger of losing by defects of character. For his hours of coldness he atones by a few minutes of exquisite dependence ; for his long fickleness—giving all his store to a total stranger and keeping ten yards between himself and his own—he makes up by falling at the right moment flat at one's feet with his paws in the air, constituting an invitation to scratch and forget that no ordinarily constituted human being can resist.

But probably the biggest gun in the deadly armoury of the Aberdeen is the art of begging. Begging is almost a birthright with an Aberdeen. It is as natural to him as to a hospital ; and he knows its power. He knows that masters and mistresses are snobs, and like to be begged to : that it is one of our foibles. This he knows, and gains immensely by it. While other dogs are fussily striving to attract attention at the table, and being told to lie down, the Aberdeen is seated quietly at the side of the weakest guest, being plied with delicacies and consuming them without a sound. The quietest Aberdeen that I ever met was at the Dorset Arms at East

Vertical and Unashamed

Grinstead, a pleasant hostelry, with Dr. Johnson's chair from the Essex Head, and signed photographs of Dan Leno, and miles of Ashdown Forest from the coffee-room window. An aged Aberdeen lives, or lived, there, who will sit motionless by your chair for hours if need be, with a look of resigned, almost pious, patience on his countenance. You never see him come in or go out. When you sit down he is not there; but suddenly he is, as still as a ghost, and to all appearances as solidly fixed in his vertical position as the Nelson Column.

Our little Boby is learning the same device. No one taught him; but one day, the time having arrived, instead of lying down as heretofore, he subsided naturally on his tail, lifted his fore-paws, and was begging. Straightway we passed utterly into his power, and he perceived it, and now in extreme cases he begs even where there is no meal in progress. For mercy, the superficial observer might think; but that is not so: no Aberdeen would beg for mercy, being in a position to command it. He begs by instinct—as the simplest way out of his difficulty; and it is so. Begging is merely one of the thousand and one wiles of this fascinating, naughty, incorrigible, and wholly adorable breed.

The Search and the Gift   *o*   *o*   *o*

THE other day I lent a lady Gaboriau's *Dossier 113*, which she returned with the remark that she liked the ingenuity of it but wished there was not so much crime. Without quite subscribing to this criticism, I think there is a good deal in it—for gentle ladies—and while meditating thereon, it occurred to me that there is an excellent opening, as the advertisements say, for a writer who will apply the principles of the detective story to blameless affairs—that is to say, retaining the detective but eliminating the bloodstains and the dark passions of Montmartre.

For, after all, the fascinating part of a detective story is not the murder or the theft, but the methods of the detective; not the poetical justice at the close, but the steps by which it has been reached. In a word, the fascinating thing about a detective story is the search.

57

The Great Seekers

The search is one of the oldest motives in literature, and it remains one of the strongest— the search either for an object or an idea—for a golden fleece, like Jason's, or a father, like Telemachus'; for definite hidden treasures, like John Silver's, or adventures that may come, like Don Quixote's or Lavengro's; for a criminal, like Lecoq's or Sherlock Holmes's, or a religion, like Lothair's; for a wife, like Cœlebs', or for position, like Evan Harrington's. These are very different examples, but the search motive is their basis, and it is the basis of half the fairy stories.

I am striking into too high a road. My original idea was that there should be a new novel of concrete search, retaining the detective and all his ingratiating methods, but retaining them only for the absorbing interest of inquiry—that alluring quality which one might call sleuthiness; and not that the cell or the gallows should claim their own. Quite the reverse, indeed; for whereas in the ordinary detective story a man is pursued in order to be punished, in the new detective story he might be tracked in order to be rewarded. No matter why the detective was engaged— whether at the whim of an eccentric or by a firm of lawyers to find an heir—his methods need not differ. All his gifts of deduction, his disguises, his resource, his godlike opportunism, that we find so irresistible, might be retained; but his revolver and handcuffs—those, I fear, would go. Their absence would not, however, impair the search—and the search is the thing.

But my scheme would do more than merely satisfy the reader's craving for excitement. It would automatically bring back the novel of character, the novel of adventure on the road among men and women of to-day — the real romance. Let us take an example to illustrate what I mean; and it happens that the very lady who made the criticism which started me on these meditations supplies what I want. With the returned copy of Gaboriau's story came a present of an old sampler—very restful to look upon, with its faded silks all sobered by time into soft neutral tints, and a primitive representation of the Tree of Knowledge flanked by our first parents, the serpent intervening. Above are these verses, spelt in a pre-Rooseveltean day:—

> "Jesus, permit thy grarachious name to stand
> As the first effots of my youthful hand,
> And as my little fingers over the canvas move,
> Engage my tender heart to seak thy love,
> With thy dear children have a part,
> And wright my name myself upon Jesusis heart."

At the foot is written—

"Hariot Pickin worked this sampler June 2, aged 13, 1828."

Instructions to a Detective

Now, what could be a better task to set a detective than to find Hariot Pickin or her descendants? She was thirteen in June 1828: that is to say, if alive to-day she is an old lady of ninety-two. Did she marry? If so, her name probably ceased to be Pickin. No doubt the tracking of Hariot would not take very long; but several things about it are certain. One is that the *modus operandi* of the discoverer would be interesting, and the other is that his inquiries would of necessity take him among many persons, and would, faithfully recorded, make excellent reading. I often find myself pining a good deal for the old-fashioned kind of novel in which there are long journeys, and in which new characters are continually appearing. The search for Hariot Pickin, in capable hands, should yield much satisfaction of this kind.

Another example. I turn to my shelves and take down an old book. It is Bunyan's *Holy War*, in calf, much stained and battered. On the fly-leaf, in a very faint ink, is written "David Sandeman"; on the top of the introduction, also in very faint ink, "Wm. Bathgate." "Bring me," suppose I were to say to the detective, "as soon as you can, full particulars of this David Sandeman and this William Bathgate." Would it not be an interesting task? Would not the record of his adventures be full of human nature? Probably there have been so many David Sandemans and William Bathgates that he could not do it; but it serves as an example, and in this kind of story failure is of little importance, since the real thing is the people by the way. Anything that can multiply good novels of people by the way is to be desired.

But I have still a third example. When I reached my modest home the other evening, I found a parcel and a letter. The letter had neither beginning nor end, nor had it any address; it merely said, in a firm and generous hand, that the writer, having gathered from certain printed words of mine that I like the good things of the earth (when I can get them!), and having also a feeling that the pleasure that she had drawn from these and other printed words of mine ought to be repaid a little, was leaving at my door two packets of caravan-borne tea which had come to her from Russia, and which she liked to think her friends were drinking—she herself, she added, adhering the while to her customary half-crown blend.

Now, here was a pretty thought and a pretty deed! Of caravan-borne tea I had often heard, but had never drunk any, much less owned it. And of gratitude I had often occasionally heard whisperings, but not much of that does one meet

with either. Yet here were both together! Well,
I drank the tea, and it was exquisite; but the
trouble—the little drop of bitter in the teacup—
was how was I to say " thank you" for it. I
suppose, logically speaking, I had been saying
" thank you" for a long time, putting the cart
before the horse, so to speak : so at least the
lady's kind-hearted letter indicates with such
grace. But who would be logical? I wanted to
say it again.

Of course I did nothing; but here was a chance
for a search-novel all to hand. To find that Lady
Bountiful! I might, of course, have stumbled on
the trail instantly; and it might have taken years.
Sherlock Holmes, I suppose, would have placed
her letter under the microscope; he would have
analysed the ink; he would have carried a little
sample of the tea to the Docks—possibly even to
Russia. How interesting it would all be!

So I have never been able to say " Thank you."
Not until now.

And yet will She read this book also, or have I
outstayed my welcome ? .

A Philosopher that Failed ✍ ✍ ✍

OF Oliver Edwards, nothing, I believe, is known beyond the fact that he had been at Pembroke College with Dr. Johnson; that he was a solicitor in Barnard's Inn; that he married twice; that he lived on a little farm of sixty acres near Stevenage and came to London twice a week; and that he wore grey clothes and a wig with many curls, and went to church on Good Fridays. We know of Edwards' life only this, and of his speech we have only some dozen sentences; and yet he will live for ever, by virtue of having crossed the stage of literature on one fine morning one hundred and twenty-nine years ago. He might be likened to the bird with which the Venerable Bede compared the life of man in a famous and beautiful passage: the bird that flies out of the dark void into the lighted banqueting hall and out again into the void once more. So with Edwards · for sixty years he was not; then

63

he met Dr. Johnson and his Boswell in Butcher Row, stayed with them for an hour; and was not again. But the hour was sufficient: it gave him time to make his one deathless remark. By virtue of that remark he lives, and will live.

Edwards's day was Good Friday, April 17, 1778—"a delightful day," says Boswell. How little the good Edwards can have thought, as he climbed out of his bed in Barnard's Inn that morning and donned his grey clothes and his curly wig, that he was about to become immortal. He spent, I take it, the early hours in his office, reading conveyances or deeds and writing letters; then he went to church, whither Dr. Johnson and Boswell had also gone, to St. Clement's, which through some strange stroke of luck is standing, with the Doctor's pew intact within it, to this dark, irreverent, rebuilding day.

On the way Boswell (who could grow the flower quite easily now, having obtained much seed) remarked that Fleet Street was the most cheerful scene in the world, adding, skilfully as he thought, "Fleet Street is, in my mind, more delightful than Tempe!" The Doctor, however, having the same dislike of the imitator that most teachers and all cynics possess, had his dash of cold water ready. "Ay, ay, but let it be compared with Mull." So they passed on to church, where the Doctor was pleased to see so numerous a congregation.

It was after church that they met Edwards, whom Johnson had not seen for forty years. The recognition came from the lawyer, a talkative, friendly, and not easily daunted man, who thereafter quickly got to work and enlarged to Boswell on the pleasure of living in the country. Boswell, again in the true Johnsonian manner, replied, " I have no notion of this, sir. What you have to entertain you is, I think, exhausted in half an hour." But Edwards was deeper and more sincere. "What," he said, "don't you love to have hope realised ? I see my grass, and my corn, and my trees growing. Now, for instance, I am curious to see if this frost has not nipped my fruit trees." Johnson, who had been in a reverie, possibly missing the familiar scent of incense,—for, in spite of Boswell's innuendoes to the contrary, Edwards does not appear to have been at all impressed by the magnitude and lustre of his old friend,—here remarked, " You find, sir, you have fears as well as hopes ; " and I am glad he did so, for it gave Boswell the opportunity to add the reflection, " So well did he see the whole when another saw but the half of a subject." And yet it is more than likely that Edwards saw the whole too.

The Parson's Happy Lot

Being comfortably seated in the Bolt Court library on this sunny Good Friday, Edwards, who had already commented with delightful bluntness, but perfect innocence, on the Doctor's age, remarked, "Sir, I remember you would not let us say 'prodigious' at college. For even then," he added, turning to Boswell, "he was delicate in language, and we all feared him." Johnson said nothing of this at the time, but to his Boswell said afterwards, in private, "Sir, they respected me for my literature"—meaning by "they" the undergraduates—"and yet it was not great but by comparison. Sir, it is amazing how little literature there is in the world." That was one hundred and twenty-nine years ago, and it is amazing still.

The conversation with Edwards then turned to money, and it came out that the lawyer had given much away. He also admitted to a longing to be a parson and live in comfort and comparative idleness. Johnson had an opening here, and took it. "I would rather have Chancery suits upon my hands," he said, "than the care of souls. No, sir, I do not envy a clergyman's life as an easy life, nor do I envy the clergyman who makes it an easy life." Edwards, however, did. There is no evidence that the Doctor convinced him. My impression is that he was never convinced by anyone's arguments. I picture him as the kind of man who goes through life contentedly, secure in his own opinion.

Nothing could daunt Edwards, and so innocent and happy was he that he had no notion he was not observing the strict rules of the game. The rules of the Johnson conversational game made it imperative that you should utter only questions or provocative opinions, and then wait for the answer and receive it humbly. But Edwards smilingly broke them all. He asked questions, it is true, but long before the Doctor could reply he had volunteered, with appalling hardihood, scraps of autobiography. If there is one thing an autobiographer like Johnson cannot stand it is the autobiography of others. And yet the Doctor, with his great human imagination, knew that Edwards was a pearl of sincerity and candour, and in his heart, I am sure, valued him accordingly. " I have been twice married, Doctor," said Edwards, apropos of nothing, cheerily adding the terrifying sentiment, " You, I suppose, have never known what it was to have a wife? " This—to Johnson! We can see Boswell shivering on his chair's edge. " Sir," said Dr. Johnson, " I have known what it was to have a wife, and [in a solemn, tender, faltering tone] I have known what it was to lose

a wife. It had almost broke my heart." Edwards
was unabashed. He said instantly, "How do
you live, sir?" adding, "For my part, I must
have my regular meals and a glass of good wine."
Dr. Johnson replied suitably—the kind of reply
that would usually settle the matter among
his guests—"I now drink no wine, sir. Early in
life I drank wine; for many years I drank none.
I then for some years drank a great deal."
Edwards rose to a fine height of irreverence
here, to the immense dismay, I have no doubt,
of Boswell, who, with all his advantages, had
not been at Pembroke with his hero. He cut
in with, "Some hogsheads, I warrant you." The
Doctor succeeded in taking no notice (quite possibly he was secretly flattered; we all like to be
credited with great deeds), and continued his
dull alimentary history; but the victory was
Edwards's, for the Doctor, when asked if he
ate supper, merely and very uncharacteristically
said "No," leaving it for his visitor to remark,
with something of the great man's own manner
made human, "For my part, now, I consider
supper as a turnpike through which one must
pass in order to get to bed."

That is good enough; but it is not the single
remark by which Edwards is known—on which
his deathless fame rests. That had come earlier.

Cheerfulness breaking in

"You are a philosopher, Dr. Johnson," said Edwards. "I have tried, too, in my time to be a philosopher; but I don't know how; cheerfulness was always breaking in." That was Edwards's great speech. By virtue of that candid confession he takes his place with the shining company of simple souls, the hierarchy of the ingenuous. It was too much for Boswell, who had no eye for children, young or old. But on repeating it to Mr. Burke, Sir Joshua Reynolds, Mr. Courtenay, Mr. Malone, and, indeed, all the eminent men he knew, they said with one accord that "it was an exquisite trait of character." He therefore refrained from belittling it in the book.

To Boswell's intense relief, Edwards at last went. He had begun by calling Dr. Johnson (who was sixty-nine) old; he left with another reference to his age. Looking him full in the face, he said, "You'll find in Dr. Young the line,

'O my coevals! remnants of yourselves.'"

When he was gone, Boswell came to himself again, and quickly remarked that he thought him a weak man; and the Doctor, smarting under the imputation of senility, was, I regret to say, weak enough to agree. But they were both wrong. Edwards was a strong man—strong in his cheerfulness and his transparency.

A Sketch Book ∽ ∽ ∽ ∽ ∽

I

EVER since I first read Mr. Housman's *Shropshire Lad*, that beautiful, melancholy eulogy of Nature and elegy on Man, these lines have run

> "Clunton and Clunbury,
> Clungunford and Clun,
> Are the quietest places
> Under the sun."

in my head, and "Some day," I have said, "I will go to Clun." And now I have seen Clun, and Clunton, and Clunbury (but not Clungunford), and I know that the poet is one who tells the truth. They are the quietest places under the sun.

I walked to Clun from Craven Arms, that busy junction of rails in a country of road travellers, under the shadow of Callow Hill and Wenlock Edge ; and by great good fortune I walked on a Monday morning—good fortune, because on Mondays there is an auction of cattle at Craven Arms, and faring westward then one meets little companies of sheep and lambs, and little companies of bullocks, and here a stallion, and there a bull, and carts containing jolly Shropshire farmers in front and calves under nets behind, and carts containing just jolly Shropshire farmers, and carts containing jolly Shropshire farmers in front and pigs behind, and jolly Shropshire farmers on horseback, and now and then a woman with a basket. And sometimes the sheep are driven by old men, and sometimes by boys, and sometimes by men on horseback, and once on this Monday by a gay young farmer on a bicycle, his machine being the only modern note in the day. For the rest, it was sheer Chaucer.

Thus it was all the way to Clun—or nearly all the way—nine miles, until I asked myself, "What can Clun be like after this exodus? Can there be a beast left within its walls?" A question that was answered all in good time by the sight of numberless bullocks and sheep and lambs in all the meadows that encompass that quiet place. For in this part of Shropshire the animals of the field are as the sands of the seashore.

The road lies in the valleys, one of which melts naturally into another all the way. First comes Aston-on-Clun, Clun being not only the quiet place, but also a mirthful, busy, inquisitive mill-stream with insinuating activities and a contented

purr, that keeps one company all the way here-
after—always busy and gay, and always talking
to itself. Aston-on-Clun is notable for a good
inn, with the unexpected style "The Kangaroo,"
kept, and kept genially and well, by a host and
hostess who, when they walk out together (if ever
they do), must strike dismay into the local
culverts. Then the road climbs a hill, below
which, on the left, all among the greenest water
meadows, is Clunbury, which is little more than
a great farmyard to which a church and cottages
have been added—and oh, so quiet under the
sun!

In some ways Clunbury is the quietest (always
excepting Clungunford, which I did not see),
because it is off the road, and few must be the
travellers who find it. Clunton is right in the
road; but before we enter it I must tell you of an
embarrassment. For suddenly at the side of the
road appeared the whitest, uprightest, boldest
chanticleer you ever saw, tame and friendly, and no
sooner had I done admiring him and passed on,
than there sprang from nowhere eleven hens,
white and splendid as himself, and forthwith the
whole harem, pasha and all, set out to follow
me into Clunton. I hastened my steps; they
hastened theirs: it began to be ridiculous. To
enter one of the quietest places under the sun

pursued, like the Pied Piper of Hamelin, by a crowd, not of children, but poultry, would be too absurd—apart altogether from a suggestion of theft. And so—much against my will, for there was a rare compliment here, a homage to which I am totally unused : to be followed with such affection by these dazzling aristocrats of the field —so I shoo'd them back, and passed through Clunton unattended, just the ordinary, insignificant creature that I am, without retinue or the adoration of fowls ; and so on to the goal.

Clun, I may say at once, has all the necessaries of life. It has a river, and a grey bridge, and a church half-way up the hill, and a castle high on its green mound, with noble stonework still remaining, and a hospital for old men, such as Anthony Trollope's Warden had in his care, each old man having to wear a cap and gown in Clun's few but important streets ; and several inns, of which, remembering good fortune at Aston-on-Clun, I made choice of " The Buffalo." And while the meal was preparing I sat on a seat in the sunny garden on a southern slope, and watched the smoke stealing up from the chimneys beyond the river below, and heard the sleepy sounds from the timber yard, and now and then a dog barked or a cock crew, and now and then someone crossed the bridge, not because he had any business to do—oh dear, no!—but merely to get to the other side, where it might be warmer; and sitting there, I knew that the poet knew. It is the quietest place under the sun.

Some day I shall go to Clun again. For the present I am the happier for having been there.

> " Clunton and Clunbury,
>   Clungunford and Clun,
> Are the quietest places
>   Under the sun."

But what of Clungunford? It may be the best of all. Some day I shall know.

II

"TALKING of bathing," said the Captain, "I remember, years and years ago, when I was apprentice, we was lying at Sarawak. Every morning me and Fred Wynn— he was the other apprentice—we had to go a matter of a mile or so through the woods to fetch water. We carried the beaker Chinese fashion, slung to a pole acrost our shoulders. Well, the first morning, as we drew up to the spring—just a little basin of rock with the water running into it; beautiful water it was, clear as

The Golden Age.

crystal, and cold, cold as ice—as we drew up to
the spring, there was a lot of Malay girls standing
round. Girls maybe of fifteen or so—that's to
say, about our own age—and fifteen's a woman
in those hot parts. They'd been bathing, and
one was in the water when we hove in sight, and
as naked as my hand, all of 'em, except for a little
shimmy thing. Fred was for stopping, but I said,
'Come along, I mean to have a bathe.' Well,
the girls stood by laughing among themselves,
and just as I was—in a pair of trousers and
a singlet—I jumped in, splash! Lord, it nearly
cut me in two, it was that cold. You wouldn't
believe how cold it was! But we always went
in every morning, naked if we were alone, or just
as we were if the girls were there. But, bless
you, they wouldn't have minded any way.

" After a time we got quite chummy: used to
run races with them. I thought I could run in
those days: I was reckoned pretty fast. But,
bless you, those girls 'ld gather up their little
shimmy things round their waists with one hand
and run like a good-fellow. Me and Fred wasn't
nowhere.

" And afterwards we'd sling their water jugs
on the pole along with our beaker, and two or
three girls would hang on each end, and we'd
carry 'em along to just outside the village, kiss

'em good-bye all round, and then make all sail for the ship.

" Ah !" added the Captain, " they were good times."

III

" ONCE," said the detective, " I had to go to Spain to bring back an embezzler. Extradited, he was. While I was there I looked into the jail. There was an Englishman there, a sailor. 'Hullo, Jack,' I said, 'what are you here for ?' 'Why,' he said, 'they give me three years for blacking a policeman's eye.' 'No ?' I said. 'Straight !' says he. 'I'd had a drop too much one night, and the swine interfered, and I landed him a black eye. Nothing more, swelp me, and they give me three years for it.' 'Well, Jack,' I said, 'I'll see if a sovereign is any good (for I know what money can do out there), and if it is, I'll stand it.' I tried, but it wasn't no use. He was too good a man for them, I think. I went back the next day to tell him, and found him with a whip in his hand in charge of a gang of Spanish prisoners. He was lashing away all he knew. 'All right,' he said, when I told him ; 'then I'll have to stay it out, I suppose.' And he went on lamming into his men. 'I reckon I'll get quit with this country by degrees,' he said."

The Debt.

A Staffordshire Cynic

IV

As a guide to old customs and old humours the domestic pottery of England is quite trustworthy, and I recommend anyone who visits Brighton, and has time to call, to look at the Willett Collection in the Museum there. Walking idly through it lately, I was attracted by a case entitled "Conviviality," given up to jugs and mugs with snatches of song upon them, drinking mottoes, and so forth, and a pretty sprinkling of topers and maltworms and tosspots. Among this welter of flaming noses and Imperial pints my eye was caught by the "Staffordshire Beerometer," which I went to the pains of copying. Here it is :—

The Beerometer.

50. Drunk as a Lord.
45. Drunk.
40. Disguised in Liquor.
35. As sober as a man ought to be. (Knows what he is about.)
30. Drunk without, but sober within.
25. Fresh. (Worse for liquor.)
20. Market fresh. (Has had a drop.)
10. Sober as a Judge.
5. Sober as I am now. (Have had 5 quarts among three of us.)
0. Sober.
5. Had nothing since breakfast.
10. Had nothing to-day.

The Nature of a Lord

At a time when there is talk of reforming the Upper Chamber, it is pleasant to note the high-water (or should one say high-beer?) mark of the drinker's ambition. Lords, say what you will, have their use. Of course it was, to a beer-eater (as the vivid modern slang has it) in a Staffordshire pot-house the rosiest dream—to be drunk as a Lord. A Lord (whatever he may be now, and my own impression is that Lords will be Lords always) was then something so utterly splendid and ruthless: a gilt-edged creature who never walked, except from his horse or carriage into the best room of an inn, and back again; who had his way with most men and all women; who ate meat whenever he wanted it, and knew the King as a brother. That was a Lord. To be drunk like such a man as that!

At the other extreme should, but does not, come the Judge. The Apogee and the Nadir—the Lord and the Judge. But alas! it is not so. The Staffordshire satirist knew better, and below that of the Judge are two degrees of sobriety—"Sober as I am now" and "Sober." But the Beerometer is at least a hundred years old, and perhaps older. Times have changed. Judges to-day . . .

I do not consider the Beerometer to be too intelligent. It misses scores of fine shades, the *nuances* of inebriation. But for the audience for whom it was intended—the Staffordshire beer-eaters—it served. After all, to know his audience is the first essential of the rural wit. Perhaps the state at 20 degrees is the most ingenious — " market fresh "—though I prefer the commoner term (to me) of " market merry." I have always thought " market merry " one of the happiest of countryside coinages. It says everything, and says it so simply and gaily. I suppose that 30 degrees was what Terence Mulvaney had reached when he claimed to be properly sober in the head but " ondacently drunk about the legs." The condition at 35 degrees is very pleasantly stated ; but here I run risks of arousing the teetotalers, for the sentiment (with the mercury so high) cuts into their very existence. " As sober as a man ought to be " is their own motto—but at zero. To find it at 35 is the devil.

V

I MET her in Antwerp, in a saloon where English and Scotch captains, mates, and engineers could hear their own language and drink their native beverages—an odd place for a noblewoman, especially one so old and white, sprightly still, and with a

My only Baroness.

79

melancholy dignity that impressed me not a little,
and also impressed some rather too high-spirited
young people who would have made fun of her
had she abated a jot of this birthright.

It was two in the morning when she entered,
with a large book under her arm and in her hand
a bundle of tickets. The tickets were for a
concert she was giving, and I bought one,
although it was not till the next week, when I
should be far away ; and then she told me she
was a poet, and we sat down together at a little
table, and she opened her book and read to me
with fond maternal *empressement* a number of
very indifferent sonnets copied there in her thin,
angular, foreign hand. Interspersed among the
sonnets were letters from the great men to whom
she had sent them : all Frenchmen, and all very
polite to Madame la Baronne ; and a few
cuttings, chiefly from small local Belgian papers,
referring to her concert platform triumphs. She
told me her history, too, but I forget it ; and a
few audacious stories, but I forget those too.
Her, however, I shall not forget, with her white
head and her wistful air of decayed gentility, and
the occasional hint of impropriety in her tired eye,
and her manuscript book of weak verse and in-
sincere compliments. I remember her because
she was exceptional, but also because she was

simple; and I know I made her happy because when she shuffled out to carry her tickets to another saloon I kissed her finger-tips and gave her such a bow as never before or since have I called on my poor back to execute.

VI

IT is in a sailing-boat that I would choose always to approach Beaulieu. It was thus the last time I saw her—the perfect day. We had come across from the Island under a fresh breeze, our ears filled with the rush of our progress, and the sibilant wake of the little dinghy tugging at its rope behind, and all the murmuring of sails and cordage amid light-hearted waves and wind. That in itself is good enough; and then suddenly we had turned into the invisible Beaulieu River, as still as a pond, and had crept inland between fields and trees as silently as the flight of a distant bird save for the dinghy's contented chuckle.

The sea for the great emotions—the high romance, the supreme carelessness; but there is a minor romance about a river that in its way is equally fascinating. It is the difference between the high road and the footpath. If I had a yacht of my own, I would always be sailing up new

Beaulieu River.

rivers. To sail up a new river is almost more of
an enterprise than to set one's prow towards the
illimitable ocean. To be so near humanity, yet
apart from it; to thread one's way in strange
landscapes; to pass through towns one has never
seen before, perhaps not stopping at all; to see
men and women on the banks for the first and
last time at once—old men, lovers, children. I
am thinking now of the great rivers that are
navigable far inland; but the Beaulieu River,
though very short and very lonely, has its
romance too. It leads inland!

A house or so at the mouth, a farm a little
higher on the left, are all its signs of life until one
comes to Buckler's Hard; the rest is meadows,
trees, and birds. Birds all the way; for on the
first boom that marks the entrance channel
a shag was perched motionless with extended
wings, like a fowl in heraldry. At one bend we
surprised a heron, who flapped off cumbrously,
old enough and wise enough to have trusted us;
curlews were playing their plaintive reed instru-
ments almost without cessation; plovers ran
along the banks; and once a swan bustled five
grey cygnets into safety as we came into sight.

By its birds and its verdant flatness the Beaulieu
River reminded me not a little of the Broads; but
the Broads have nothing like Buckler's Hard.

The Secret of Buckler's Hard

Buckler's Hard stands alone — quite the most curious village or hamlet I ever saw. It is more like a short section of a Georgian High Street than anything else—cut out of some quiet old market town like Lymington, near by, and set bodily on the top of a bank in a field by the side of a serene river. It begins suddenly and ends suddenly, climbing the slope indeed to the sky; the backs of the houses that form the two sides of the street looking upon illimitable greenery, the fronts facing each other across a roadway that is grass. With the exception of the first house on the right-hand side, all are about the same size; but this one is more imposing than the others, and has a doorway that might have come from Bedford Row. I puzzled some time over Buckler's Hard, where we disembarked and loitered, and then the secret was given me by a tall fisherman busy with his nets on the bank. There was once a dockyard here, and the houses were the homes of the shipwrights, and the imposing one at the end was that of the chief officer. Nelson's *Agamemnon* was built here, the fisherman told me . . . and as he spoke it was possible in the hot noon air to hear again the hammers and all the myriad noises of this noblest and bravest of industries.

The Beating of the Hoofs ∽ ∽ ∽

HAVING occasion the other day to post from Brecon to Abergavenny, I was particularly gratified to find that the landlady of the " Castle " had put at our disposal a carriage with rubber tyres and a pair of horses; for I knew that we were thus destined to have the best of music all the way—the beating of the hoofs. And it was so. Silent or talking, thoughtful or observant of the mountains beneath their grey hoods, I was ever conscious of the sound of eight loyal and urgent iron-shod feet — not so fiercely as one hears it in the background of one of the movements of Raff's " Léonore " symphony, but a steady, soothing undertone.

It is not the least of the advantages of the rubber tyre, that this pleasant melody is so clarified. It is perhaps the best thing that Leopold, King of the Belgians and Despot of the Congo, has done. Before rubber tyres came in, one had to go to the horse tramways for it; and I remember how agreeable, in consequence, were the long rides up the Hampstead Road and the Brecknock Road that I took when first I came to London. But the hoofs on the Welsh macadam were better than this, for they were steady and sure; there were none of those sudden and disconcerting mishaps that are so common on London's greasy stones —those agonised slippings of the iron shoe with a catastrophic clamour to which not even the oldest Londoner's ear ever quite becomes accustomed.

I will not name the absence of hoof-beats in so many words as a count in the indictment of the motor-car, because the indictment of the motor-car must be getting to be very teasing reading; but I will say that the car has certainly a very regrettable immunity from hoof-beats, and has nothing for the ear in their place. For the ear nothing: but I suppose that the increased speed that the petrol offers is, for most, sufficient compensation. Not, however, for me, who have an old-fashioned notion that for the high road, as opposed to a track or rails, the speed that horses may attain is speed enough. The glory of motion as celebrated by De Quincey is as much of that glory as most of us sinners are entitled to. I have an uneasy feeling that I have not earned the right to dash along at twenty-five to thirty-five

miles an hour,—that we ought not to go faster
than the horse,—although I should be puzzled to
say exactly what it was I had left undone that
would qualify me to do so. But the feeling is
there, none the less, and it is none the weaker
for being vague.

What I sometimes wonder is, would De
Quincey, were he able to sit beside Mr.
Jarrott, or that terrible Belgian, Jenatzy,
have an increased sense of speed, or would he
still pin his faith to horses to convey most profoundly the impression of velocitous travel?
Because it is not, of course, always the fastest
thing that most suggests fastness. A moderately
hasty omnibus, for example, rolling down Whitehall, would seem to be moving with a greater
impetus than the hansom that overtook it : and I
can conceive it possible that a runaway stage coach,
going at only fifteen miles an hour, might have a
far more impressive onset than a motor-car going
at forty miles an hour, under perfect control.
If so, that would justify De Quincey.

But the comparison would be fair only if the
observer were horse-blind. It would be the horse
that would really convey the impression of speed ;
not the speed itself. The speed of a motor-car,
even at forty miles an hour, one would not notice
very vividly unless one were in its wind, so to

speak ; but the speed of four horses plunging along, out of control, with a coach of people behind them, would seem to be terrific, because the eye would be trebly fed : fed with the actual quickness of the vehicle, so much quicker than usual ; fed with the alarm of the passengers ; but most of all fed with the fury and appalling madness of energy of the animals themselves, all so frantic and undisciplined. I have not seen many runaway horses, but all that I have seen filled me with a tightening alarm that I can still recall with the utmost vividness.

I doubt if a sculptor or painter, challenged to represent the most sublimely terrifying thing that human beings can meet, could do better than to mould or depict a frenzied horse. I believe that the horse is not only the noblest animal we know, but in its rage the most terrible. It is customary to say that the lion is the noblest creature, but the lion, for all his grandeur, has a furtive look ; and the tiger even more so ; while the elephant, for all his size, has just that touch of the grotesque which is fatal. But the horse is beautiful, and noble too. And it is all to his advantage as a symbol of terror that he is normally the kindly friend of man, in perfect subjection, and that his frenzy is an aberration. The contrast intensifies the emotion.

The Incomplete Philippian

I should, however, be conveying a very false impression if these remarks upon the noble animal led anyone to suppose that I am either a horseman or even comfortable in a horse's presence. Quite the reverse. I am one to whom the horse is an unknown and perilous quantity. I have for horses and dogs an affection that most people seem to keep for their fellow-men; but although with dogs I am at home, I am totally at a loss to know how to deal with the larger creature. A horse's eye disquiets me: it has an expression of alarm that may at any moment be translated into action. I like to know where an animal is looking, and these bright, startled, liquid convexities never tell me.

I have been on a horse's back, it is true. I once hired a horse and rode it over the South Downs for a fortnight; but I never feel that there is true *rapport* between a horse and myself. I began too late. To understand horses and be understood by horses, one must be brought up with them. But for the great centaurs—the giants of the saddle—no one can have more admiration than I: a little, perhaps, because they are so foreign, almost so astral, a people. I don't mean jockeys, who are mere riding automata without personalities; I mean the great hunting men with the noble and resonant names,

—and of all of whom " characteristic anecdotes "
(brave words!) are told,—the men celebrated by
the glowing pen of "Nimrod" : Tom Assheton-
Smith, and Hugo Meynell, and Sir Bellingham
Graham, and Tom Sebright, and Mr. Osbaldeston,
and Jack Musters, and John Mytton, and John
Warde of Squerries.

When one reads the lives of the ordinary great
men — statesmen, poets, divines, painters, and
so forth—one can to a considerable extent put
oneself in their place : the life described, although
carried out to a high power, is still more or less
one's own, is recognisable. But to read "Nimrod's"
generous and spirited pages—to read of these
mighty and wonderful horsemen—is (with me)
to be transported to a kind of fairyland to which
I am never likely really to penetrate, and where,
if I did, I should be an alien and ashamed. That
is why I think " Nimrod " one of the greatest of
writers—because he takes me into an unattain-
able world and keeps me enchanted.

" When Jack Shirley was whipper-in to Mr.
Smith, he was riding an old horse called Gadsby
(not much the better for having been many years
ridden by his master) over one of the worst fields
in Leicestershire for a blown horse—between
Tilton and Somerby—abounding with large ant-
hills and deep, holding furrows. The old horse
was going along at a good slapping pace, with

his head quite loose, and downhill at the time, whilst Jack was in the act of putting a lash to his whip, *having a large open clasp knife between his teeth at the time!*"

That is the kind of thing that "Nimrod" tells, and what could be more different from the ordinary routine of a literary man!

Or take Captain Bridges of the Hambledon Hunt:—

"Being out one day with the foxhounds, he saw two gentlemen parleying with a farmer in a gateway, who refused to let them pass through it. The Captain rode up to them, and asked what was the matter. 'Why,' said one of the gentlemen, 'this farmer says he will murder the first man who attempts to go into his field.' 'Does he?' said the Captain; 'then here goes, life for life,' and immediately charged him. The fellow aimed a desperate blow at his head with a very heavy stick, which, in spite of the velvet cap, would have felled him to the ground, if he had not had the good fortune to have avoided it; when, taking to his heels, the coward fled, with the Captain after him, and absolutely crept into a large covered drain to avoid him. 'Who-whoop!' said the Captain, 'I've run him to ground, by G—d!'"

"Nimrod" tells us, later, in proof of the Captain's humour, that the last time he saw him out he told him he had been severely attacked by gout in the early morning, but, "determined to hunt," he had taken two strong calomel pills and sixty drops of colchicum; on the top of this he had put a glass of hot gin and water on the road to covert, "to keep things in their place." There's a captain for you! It was of this gallant sportsman, by the way, that "Nimrod" uses the admirably descriptive phrase: "the nightingale had oftener heard him than he had the nightingale."

A tired journalist, worn with town, looking out for a hero, an exemplar—could he do better than choose Captain Bridges? Yet how impossible!

But of the harum-scarum hunting man Mytton is the blazing example. Even less like the daily routine of a journalist and literary hack was the career of this inspired rake-hell, who thought so little of money that he could be traced in his morning walks by dropped bundles of banknotes; who fought dogs with his teeth, on equal terms, and won; who drank six bottles of port daily, the first while shaving; who spent £10,000 in getting into Parliament, and occupied his seat only half an hour; who consented to go to Oxford only on condition that he was never asked to open a book; who jumped toll-gates in his gig; who owned and hunted two packs, and once came in at the death, after many hours' riding, with three broken ribs;

who set a spring trap for his chaplain one Sunday
morning, and, having caught him, thought the
frolic amply atoned for by a bottle of Madeira;
who thrashed all who offended him, and afterwards
gave them a guinea; and who, when some kind
of compromise was offered him by his lawyer
which would save an estate from the hammer and
produce him an income of £6000 a year, remarked,
" I wouldn't give a damn to live on £6000 a
year." Surely if unlikelihood of imitation is a
measure of admiration (as it is), here is a hero
indeed for a quill-driver who must keep office
hours!

Ever since I can remember I have been
fascinated by the life of John Mytton, although
there is no real pleasure to be taken in it. The
spectacle of the riotous spendthrift, the man
whose only enemy is himself, as we say, is melancholy enough, however we consider it. Why not,
then, leave poor Mytton's ghost unvexed? Because,
I would say, he was great. In his way he was
among the giants. England has produced many
madcaps, many wastrels of genius: to go the pace
recklessly, to sow wild oats, seeming to be more
easy with our youth than with those of any nation,
the result probably of security and wealth and the
absence of that enforced military service which
reminds the young Continental so forcibly that he

A Furious Career

is but a cog in a great machine, together with a certain tendency in the national character (observed once very acutely by Falstaff) to overdo our amusements.

It is not so long since Mytton died : 1834—the same year in which died Charles Lamb. He was born in the year that saw Lamb contributing poems to Coleridge's first volume, 1796, and it is not uninteresting to reflect how different were the two lives that were simultaneously to pass in London and at Halston, Mytton's home in Shropshire. Mytton's father died when his son was two, and probably the boy's ruin was a result, for his mother was fond to folly, and no one opposed his will. He went to Westminster and Harrow, being expelled from both, and came of age to £60,000 in ready money and an income of £10,000. For a short time he was a cornet in the 7th Hussars, but on his majority he resigned, and took to country pursuits. It was in 1819 that he brought himself to sit in Parliament for half an hour ; in 1820 came the dissolution, and he legislated no more. He married twice—his first wife died, and his second left him. His hounds, his racehorses, his cellars, his coverts, and his friends all did their work, and by 1830 he was a debtor in hiding in Calais. In 1834 he was dead of delirium tremens in the King's Bench Prison. He was buried in

the private chapel of his old home, and his funeral
was attended by half Shropshire, for the country-
people idolised him. His life was written by his
friend " Nimrod," who also had come upon disaster,
although not so luridly, and was also a refugee at
Calais. It is a curious, warm-hearted, tolerant
book, unique in the language—the kindest
biography that a rake-hell ever had, and a
wonderful memorial of the three-bottle days that
are past. Now and then the gallant " Nimrod "
sweats something very like blood in his efforts to
palliate his friend's enormities, but he almost
succeeds.

Mytton, looked at from one point of view, was
just a criminal detrimental, wickedly selfish,
shamelessly wasteful. That is true enough.
But he rose to such heights in this wastefulness,
and he gave himself to folly with such generous
abandon, that he compels admiration. His follies,
indeed, were (as often happens) largely runaway
virtues. Bravery in the hands of a young fool
quickly becomes recklessness; generosity turns
to extravagance; conviviality degenerates into
drunkenness. Mytton had none of the petty
vices, the dirty little mean self-protective
thoughts that seem to be consistent with the
highest reputations. He was open and without
arrière pensée. Having well thrashed an opponent,

he gave him (as I have said) a guinea. With
more judgment he would have been a great
country gentleman. Instead, he is perhaps the
biggest madcap fool in English history.

He was certainly the only one whose life was
published with aquatints by Alken and Rawlins.
Those aquatints—how well I remember them!
I saw the book first—where, I forget now—when
I was quite a child, and some of the pictures
burned their way into my memory. John Mytton
returning from Doncaster races in a chaise with
the windows open—I should remember that
nightpiece for ever, even if in counting his
winnings he was not amused to see the wind catch
the banknotes and whirl them into the void.
John Mytton riding his bear into the drawing-
room, to the consternation of his guests. Who
that first saw that picture in childhood could
ever forget it? Mytton was very amusing with
this bear, and once, after making George
Underhill, the horse-dealer, exceedingly drunk,
he put him to bed with it and two bulldogs.
(He had an inexhaustibly pretty fancy.) John
Mytton forcing the leader of his tandem to jump
a gate, but being foiled by the wheeler. John
Mytton shooting ducks on the ice under the
moon, crawling after them in nothing but his
night-shirt, gun in hand. John Mytton setting

this same night-shirt, or another, on fire to cure the hiccoughs.

And lastly, the spirited picture of the famous incident of the guest and the gig, by which, in many persons' minds, Mytton lives. " Was you ever much hurt of being upset in a gig ? " asks the genial John of a friend whom he is driving in one of those vehicles. " No, thank God," says the unsuspecting man, forgetting with whom he had to deal, " for I never was upset in one." " What," replied Mytton, " never upset in a gig ? What a damned slow fellow you must have been all your life ! " and, " running his near wheel up the bank, over they both went." The story contains John Mytton's greatness. The superb foolhardiness of it ; the excellent *bonhomie* of it ; the swiftness of the catastrophe, impulse and action being one ; the recklessness not only of his own life, but his friend's, for the prosperity of the joke :—these would be impossible to a small man.

Had Mytton been a soldier, with such a disregard of danger and rapidity of thought and deed, his monument might be at this moment in St. Paul's Cathedral and his statue in Trafalgar Square —and he no different in character. But fate designed that he should squander his gifts and do no one the faintest service. More, it was admitted

A Nut for Optimists

by his biographer that Mytton was drunk for seven years on end, a term extended to twelve years by another witness. There is here a waste of power and a perversion of fine, generous instincts that I leave to Dr. Pangloss and other apologists for this universe to explain away.

Our Gardeners and Luck of the Woods

I SAY "our gardeners," but it is a misnomer. I believe that, strictly speaking, we have never had a gardener at all. We have had only substitutes, understudies, "supplies." A gardener, I am told, before you can rightly call him "your gardener," must be in your service only; whereas our gardeners have been independent men whom gold has for a while bribed into spending a few of their hours each week on our soil, and that only irregularly, and who have instantly thrown us over when anything better offered.

However, let it pass. Our gardeners they shall be called.

We have had so many that I forget their order; but let us begin with Banks. Banks was an old, cheery man with a short white beard—a widower, who lived all alone in a tiny cottage that might have been inhabited by a witch in a fairy tale. Once I went to see him there—when

he was ill with jaunders (as he called them), and
found him in bed as yellow as a dandelion. You
have no idea how funny an old yellow gardener
in bed can look. Banks was a good workman,
and a very kindly personage to have about the
place, and he would have become our real
gardener, I think, had it not been for an act of
folly on his own part which removed him from
our neighbourhood for ever. His exit was
dramatic, for one morning he was sent into the
village to buy some cord, and he was not heard of
again for six weeks, and then he was in a distant
town, with his only son, and was not in his right
mind. And when the truth came out the case
was harder than ever. To think that Cupid
should have had an eye to that odd little old
man! But he had, and the odd little old man
fell—rather heavily—and he was seen no more.
By Heaven's mercy the baby died.

That was the end of Banks, and no more did
he brighten our garden with his merry old face
and delight our ears with his odd words, of which
the verb " to brish " was by no means the last—
to brish being something midway between really
cutting a hedge and just looking at it.

After Banks came, I think, Rateman—or was it
Thrupp? No, Rateman. Rateman was younger
and more energetic than Banks, but not so good.

He dashed at his work, and made vast superficial differences to the place; but it was not thorough work. He never trenched two spits deep in his life, and never will; whereas Banks would not have slept if he had done less where it was needed. Rateman wanted to cut down trees and move mountains, while Banks was content to help Nature do her gentle, gradual will. Another difference between Rateman and Banks was that whereas Banks always had money, Rateman always wanted it. I have borrowed money from Banks, but Rateman still owes me two shillings. It was immediately after acquiring that sum that he left.

Peters came next. Peters was by profession a poacher, but he affected gardening as a blind to the police. He yawned most of the day from want of sleep, and yet worked too, and not at all badly. Peters had the artistic temperament, and our garden, in which are no vegetables—nothing but flowers and shrubs and odd levels and much stonework—pleased him and drew out his fancy. We lost Peters only because the iron hand of circumstances caused him to move.

Then came our greatest failure—a decrepit old man with the horrible name of Crossbones. Those other men had all done something, even if it were not what we wanted done; but Crossbones did nothing but patient and ineffectual hoeing. He had a stock phrase with which to meet all suggestions: "I've never done that in gennlemen's places," his illusion being that he had spent a protracted lifetime as the honoured gardener of this and that aristocrat. For all I know to the contrary, he may have done so; but he gave us none of the benefit of his career. As the leisurely disturber of the topmost soil of a "gennleman's place" he was perfection; but beyond that he was useless. He quickly went.

Thrupp, who succeeded, plunged us into difficulties, as you will see. Thrupp was a strong man of powerful will, with a contempt for his employers. No matter what he was told, he did only what he thought right. For he looked upon himself as one who could make no mistake, and his standard was the wonderful plot of land behind his own cottage, of whose fruitfulness and docility he was never tired of telling us. There was nothing this garden did not bring forth—its soil was everything it should be, short of auriferous. Thrupp took no stock in flowers, and at last, by dangling before our eyes a promise of some such fecundity as his own being persuaded by his gifted hands to grace a piece of our land, he induced us to allow him to turn half the orchard into a vegetable patch. But nothing was

ever grown there but crowsfoot—plenty of it—
and nettles that sting most infernally when one
goes to pick up walnuts and apples. I knew in
my heart that this would be so; but Thrupp was
master. How he came to leave us we have no
real knowledge; but I am sure he never received
notice, because I am sure we should never have
had the courage to give it—having no telephone.
But vanish he did, and very characteristically; and
since we did not know whether he had left or
not, and as we were terrified by what might
happen if we engaged another man and Thrupp
was only resting, we were for several weeks
without any help at all. I sent out scouts to
learn what he was doing, but could get no real
information. They could not definitely report
that he was in another situation. I wrote him
postcards, but he did not answer. I would have
called but for want of courage and his eye. . . .
That cold eye. . . .

I forget who came next, but there were several
stop-gaps before Coward appeared, one of whom,
I remember, advised me to pay a shilling or two
more the next time I bought a spade; and another
carefully pulled up some scores of cherished
seedlings under the impression that they were
weeds. And then the millennium dawned; for,
taking everything into consideration, Coward (who

is still with us) is the most successful man we have
had, for he works well, obeys instructions, dis-
tinguishes between weeds and seedlings, is willing
to do anything else if need be, has no dignity to
incommode him, and does not talk unless he is
spoken to. Also he is without theories, and
breeds rather good ducks. His drawback is a
fondness for golf (he is a local champion), which
deprives us of his services far too often. When
he is most wanted here, he is on the links.

One peculiarity of Coward's is perhaps worth
mentioning. Although very strong, he has the
thinnest arms I ever saw on anyone but a *première
danseuse*—thinner even than hers, maybe, for I sus-
pect that much of the thinness of Genée's arms,
for example, is illusory, proceeding from the contrast between them and her exceedingly sturdy
legs. Such legs ! Have you ever seen Genée ? Half
fairy, half kitten, and wholly adorable. But we
are talking about gardeners. Coward's arms, as
I say, for all his power, are thin as hop-poles. But
his most interesting characteristic is his wayside
fortune—he has what I will call the luck of the
woods. If anything curious or untoward is afoot,
Coward is there ; if *raræ aves* are seen by anyone,
the eyes are Coward's.

The other Sunday, for example, I had an
appointment with him ; and as it was Sunday

afternoon, he had on his best clothes, and I noticed that not only his light grey suit, but also his dark grey overcoat, were those which I had given him a few months ago, and once again I wondered why one can ever be so foolish as to give away such valuable and irreplaceable things as old clothes.

Well, we talked for some time—an hour—on the matter in hand, and then he turned to go (he lives two miles away, across the common), but swinging round again, he remarked casually, "I picked up a woodcock as I came along." "Yes," I said tentatively, expecting that he was proposing to hand it to me as an offering to the table, and wondering what it had died of. "Rather a good one," he added, and, throwing open his coat—my coat—revealed the head and three inches of bill of a large woodcock protruding from an inside pocket : to my astonishment intensely alive. Its sparkling black eyes looked at me with a steady inquisitiveness, but no fear. Coward pulled it forth, quite naturally and easily, as if live woodcocks were his normal cargo, and began to stroke its head as affectionately and gently as if the soul of his grandam had really taken up its habitation therein ; and the bird accepted the attention quietly and, to all appearance, happily. I was then told that it had a broken wing ; was probably shot the day before ; and was now on its way to the keeper's. The bird was then put back into the pocket—my pocket—again, and its captor walked off, leaving me all amused perplexity.

I was not only perplexed and amused ; I was sad too. I had a sense of failure. For a large part of the force of this anecdote is that that overcoat was no longer mine. So long as I owned it and wore it, nothing ever got into its pockets but such dull and normal articles as pipes and pouches and gloves. But no sooner had I given it away than one of the shyest and strongest of British birds found its way there quite naturally.

The reason is, of course, not only that the coat had ceased to be mine, but that I had given it to a man eminent among those who have the luck of the woods. Such luck cannot be acquired ; you have it or you have it not, like the *ars poetica* or a caul. No matter how much you want it, you cannot get it. A man who has it not may spend his whole life in the country and never even come across a blind-worm ; a man who has it may live all his life in Bloomsbury and one day visiting Epping Forest find a cuckoo's egg in a robin's nest.

I don't say I am totally without it, because

Shadow without Substance

I was once with a man who has it strongly, and saw a pigeon attacked in mid-air by a hen-harrier and killed; and it fell near us, and turned out to be a carrier pigeon with a message under its wing and a registered number, which led to an interesting correspondence. This shows that I am not wholly destitute of such luck, because if I were I should not have been walking with that man. But I do not possess more than a glimmering, although I once found a black snake wriggling across Great Portland Street at eleven o'clock on a Sunday night, and killed it with a ground ash; and although one Sunday morning three years ago I was confronted suddenly by a young owl on a juniper bush, and it allowed me to take it in my arms. But these experiences are exceptions, proving no rule. The man who has the luck of the woods always has it, like my gardener friend, to whom gravitate, by a kind of natural law, all creatures in distress, and before whose eyes are unfolded the most interesting dramas that the English fauna can play. Such men have the key of the countryside.

As I say, we had been talking for an hour before he showed me his treasure-trove. Here came out the difference between us—between a man who has the luck of the woods and a man who has it not; because, had I chanced on

a woodcock with a broken wing, I should in the
first place never have thought of packing it in my
pocket, and, in the second place, it would have
been the first thing I should have spoken of on
meeting an acquaintance.

Those who possess the luck of the woods, the
key of the countryside, are very enviable. To
me they are more enviable than any other men
—more enviable even than conjurers.

Conjurer and Confederate ∽ ∽ ∽

AMBITION takes men very differently. This would enter Parliament, and That would have a play accepted at the Court; This would reach the North Pole, and That would live at Chislehurst; while a fifth would be happy if only he had a motor-car. Speaking for myself, my ambition has always been to have a conjurer perform under my own roof, and it has just happened. I obtained him from the Stores.

No one, I suppose, will be taken in by the statement that I was engaging this wizard for the children; it was really for myself. Much as the children enjoyed his tricks and his banter (so fascinating, as one of his testimonials said, to the family of the Countess of ——), it was I who enjoyed him most, because I helped him with his preparations; saw him unpack his wonderful bags and lay the sacred paraphernalia on the table;

procured for him such articles as he required; and so forth. I have never been so near magic before. Like all great men when one comes closely in touch with them, he was quite human, quite like ourselves: so much so, indeed, that in addition to his fee he wanted his cab fare both ways. It is very human to want things both ways.

I have been wondering how long it would take me to learn to be a conjurer, and if it is not too late to begin. I used to meditate a course of billiard lessons from one of the great players, but I gave that up long ago. I realised that a man who wants to play billiards must have no other ambition. Billiards is all. But one might surely in the course of a winter acquire something more than the rudiments of conjuring, and I would pay a guinea a lesson with pleasure. I don't want to be a finished conjurer. I merely want to do three tricks with reasonable dexterity. Of course, if one can do three tricks one can do thirty, but it is three and three only I have in mind. (1) I want to borrow a watch and put it in a pestle and mortar and grind it to powder and then fire a pistol at a loaf of bread and find the watch whole again in the midst of the crumb. (2) I want to borrow a tall hat and throw in flour and break eggs into it and stir it all up, and hold it over a spirit lamp for a second, and then produce a beautiful warm cake. (3) I want to find hens' eggs in old men's beards and little girls' hair. Tricks with cards and money and so forth I don't mind about, because I would always rather see them done than do them — there is such fascination in the clean, swift movements of the conjurer with cards, his perfect mastery of his fingers, the supple beauty of his hands. And tricks with machinery I would gladly forego.

My conjurer's most popular trick was of course that which calls upon the co-operation of a rabbit. I wrote to him in advance to insist on this. No man who at a children's party produces a live rabbit, particularly when it is very small and kicking and also black and white, is making a mistake. No matter what has gone before, this apparition will seal his popularity. The end crowns the work (as I could say in Latin if I liked). It was not only to the children that this trick was welcome, but to an elderly literary friend of mine, with whom I have collaborated more than once, and into whose life I hoped to get a little brightness by inducing him to bring the tall hat which the wizard should borrow. The thought filled him with excitement. It was bringing radiance indeed into his life to know that this old hat, which had done nothing more romantic than keep his head warm all these years, was to be used for magical purposes, and have a real rabbit extracted from it.

As with pensive melancholy I watched the conjurer packing up, he told me that he had two more performances that evening, and had been in constant request (I think I give his exact words) all through the winter months. What a life! I can think of nothing more pleasant than to live thus, continually mystifying fresh groups of people —with cab fares both ways and a satisfactory fee : to be for ever in the winter months extracting eggs from old gentlemen's beards and little girls' hair, passing cards right through one's body, catching half-crowns in the air, finding a thousand and one things in tall hats. This is to live indeed, to say nothing of the additional rapture of having a fund of facetiæ that not only ordinary children but the offspring of countesses find irresistible.

And in the summer months what does he do ? Probably he is thinking out new tricks, squandering his winter wealth (the very reverse of the bee), catching rabbits.

II. THE CONFEDERATE

" My mother has told me of fields, meadows, and hedges ; but I have never seen them. She has told me also of guns, and dogs, and ferrets,

and all the perils of the warren life ; but of these
I know nothing too. It is very unlikely that I
ever shall ; for I am in love with my art, and
will not abandon it until I must. My mother
says I must before very long, because I am
growing so fast ; but I mean to keep small. I
shall eat very little ; I eat hardly anything now.
I couldn't bear to change this wonderful career.

" This is my second winter, and I go into his
pocket quite easily still. Why should everyone
grow big ? There are dwarf men ; why not dwarf
rabbits ?

" My mother says that when I am too big I
shall just live in a hutch all day and see no one.
But I would not do that ; I would die sooner.
It is very easy to die if you want to.

" What sort of a life do you think I should
have if I could not help my master, *and knew that
another was helping him instead ?* That would be
the terrible part. Once it happened to me, when
I was ill and my brother went to a party for me.
I suffered agonies all the evening. I seemed to
hear the children laughing, and see them all
open-mouthed with amazement and rapture when
he was pulled kicking out of the empty hat. It was
terrible. I lay there sobbing and biting my claws.
But it was all right when he came back, for I
heard my master saying to his wife that *Tommy*

(that is my brother's name) was a fool. "Too heavy, too," he added, and then he brought me, with his own hands, a new crisp lettuce to see if I could eat again, and I ate it all, and have never been ill since.

"I daresay if I was an ordinary stage conjurer's rabbit I could bear old age better. But we do not do that, we go to children's parties. There is all the difference in the world.

"You have no idea how many children I see. And to hear them laugh; that is the best! I hear them laugh all the time, but I see them only for a minute or two. You must understand that until my trick comes on—and it is usually a late one—I lie all comfortable, although quivering with excitement, in my basket. I can't see, but I can hear everything. Of course I know exactly what is happening, although I can't see it. I know the order of the tricks perfectly. Now he's catching money in the air, I say to myself. Now he's finding an egg in a little girl's hair. Now he's passing cards through his body; and so on. And then comes the great moment when I hear him say, 'For my next trick I shall require the loan of a hat. Can anyone oblige me with a tall hat? As this is a rather messy trick, I don't care to use my own.' They always laugh at that; but they little think what those words are meaning

to a small black rabbit in a basket, and how my
heart is beating.

"Then the trick begins : first my master takes
out of the hat a great bunch of flags, then heaps
of flowers, then Japanese lanterns, and then a
wig. I must not tell you how this is done, but
I know ; and I must not tell you how or when I
am put into the hat, because that might lead you
to think less of my master's magic ; but after the
wig has been taken out and they are all laughing,
there is a moment . . . Then my heart seems to
stand quite still. When I come to myself I hear
my master say, 'Excuse me, sir, but you carry
very odd things in your hat. I thought the wig
was the last of them ; but here is one more.' I
cannot see the children, but I know exactly how
they are looking while he says this—all leaning
forward, with their mouths open and their eyes
so bright. And then my master takes hold of
my ears, pulls me up with a swift movement
which hurts a little, but I don't mind (mind!),
and waves me in the air. How I kick, how they
scream with delight ! 'Oh, the little darling !'
they cry. 'Oh, the sweet !' 'The pet !'

" How could I give this up ? What has life for
me without my art ?

"Sometimes when we are performing in a small
house where there is no platform, the little girls

make a rush for me and seize me from my master
and hug me and kiss me. I have been a good
deal squeezed now and then; but I know it is
because I have done well. If I had not kicked
so bravely they would not be so eager to hold me
and love me. It is homage to art. But my
master soon takes me from them and puts me in
my basket again. I am afraid he has rather a
jealous disposition."

Sister Lucie Vinken ✺ ✺ ✺ ✺

G HENT has many treasures, first of which I
suppose is that chapel at St. Bavo's which
holds enshrined "The Adoration of the Lamb,"
by Jan and Hubert Van Eyck; but looking back
on it I remember with most vividness not its
paintings or its churches, not its canals or its
Hôtel de Ville, not its streets or its ruined castle,
but Sister Lucie Vinken of the Convent of St.
Joseph in the Petit Béguinage Notre Dame.

We came to her by a kind of accident,—if
accident there be, as I like to question. It was
the Grand Béguinage that we had set out to see,
in one of those Belgian *fiacres* which, whether
you will or not, force you back to an angle of
insolent disdain. But the driver had his own
opinion, and before we knew it we were within
the gates of the older and smaller but far more
adjacent retreat, and I have since learned that in
other respects also we did well, for the Grand

All sheer Peter De Hooch

Béguinage outside the city, although very fascinating in its self-contained perfection, with its surrounding wall and little streets and squares and moats and bridges—by all accounts the ideal home for a children's commonwealth—is yet new, dating but from the eighteen-seventies, whereas the Petit Béguinage is untouched since the eighteenth century, and some of it is earlier still; and to go to Ghent to see a new building is as absurd as to go to Oxford to see a Board school.

The driver having stopped before a door in the wall with a little shrine above it, the door opened and Sister Lucie Vinken straightway became our hostess. She stood radiating welcome in a courtyard such as her countryman Peter De Hooch (for Sister Lucie Vinken is Dutch) would have painted, and drew us in. There could be no holding back, however militantly Protestant one's feelings might be, for Sister Lucie Vinken's Church does not often make a mistake, and she was not appointed to this post without reason—so charming her smile, so rosy her placid round Dutch face, so white her head-dress, and so engagingly gentle and soothing her voice. No. 233 is the number of Sister Lucie Vinken's house —all sheer Peter De Hooch too—with little bright red bricks, and white frames to the windows, and cool white walls and tiny dormers.

The others are like it, surrounding their great courtyard, which has a meadow in the midst to which have strayed from their frames, to keep Peter De Hooch in countenance these late days, half a dozen of Albert Cuyp's cows. At one end is the church, and close by is the Convent of St. Joseph, where Sister Lucie Vinken dwells and receives the curious. Long may she do so!

Sister Lucie Vinken led us first into the refectory, where each *religieuse* has a little cupboard with her own table necessaries in it, and a sliding slab on which to place them for all meals but dinner, which is taken in company at a long table. The other meals are taken separately, each sister at her cupboard. Then we went upstairs, along passages with sacred engravings on the walls, to see the bedrooms, all of which, like the houses, are dedicated to saints ; and by an odd chance, in the one that we entered, which was Lucie Vinken's own, very small and clean and holy, in one of the drawers was a packet of picture postcards of the Béguinage—only a franc —and by another chance Lucie Vinken had no change, and very naturally misunderstood me to say that it was of no importance and the balance of my five-franc piece should go to the *pauvres*. Lucie Vinken being the clever woman she is, I agreed hastily that that was what I had said.

For my Conversion

And then she enlarged upon the pleasures of the life, of which she has had three-and-twenty years, and hoped it might not be long before we were members of the same broad-bosomed Church; and indeed said that she felt it so much that if she had Madame's permission she would pray for her speedy conversion: and how can one say "No" to a request like that? And then, drawing Madame aside, she asked her in a whisper if Monsieur would resent it if she prayed also for him; and Madame assured her he would adore it: and so at this moment, for all I know, Sister Lucie Vinken is on her knees drawing me by invisible threads nearer and nearer to the Eternal City. . . . And she has my address too, for we exchanged cards, quite like duellists, and hers lies before me as I write. I have more than that; for I have her photograph, snapped as she stood in Peter De Hooch's doorway and smiled *adieu*, and not only *adieu* but *au-revoir*, as we drove away.

But I go too fast. For it was in her little bedroom, and dallying in the white passage among the sacred prints, and hovering on the stairs as we descended, that Sister Lucie Vinken told us all about these Béguinages and their history: how they were founded in the twelfth century; how the sisters were as free as air to

come and go if they wished, but mostly stayed,
all vowed to good works but not irrevocably to
anything else — teaching, nursing, sewing and
making lace, the last two employments being so
much their staple occupation as to determine the
time of vespers, which do not begin in winter or
summer until the daylight has so faded as to
endanger the workers' sight : worshipping always,
with little if any less assiduity than real nuns
who have taken the veil once and for all. " We
rise at half-past four," she said in her quiet
voice. " We are all very sleepy, yes, but since it
is to adore the good God it gives us pleasure."
Béguinages, Lucie Vinken added, are to be found
in the other chief Belgian towns—Louvain has
a very beautiful one—but Ghent is their capital.
Ghent counts her Béguines in thousands : the
others only in hundreds. And so on.

And as she talked I found myself wondering
if the Béguinage could ever come to this country,
where unemployed unmarried women darken the
earth. And as I looked out of a window and
watched the quiet figures standing alone or in
company at their gateways, all contented-looking
and ready to smile in an unsmiling country—for
the Belgian face is hard—or moving about by the
church and the meadow, talking to their friends
from the city, playing with children (which they

may have to stay with them if they like), and returning from sickbeds and other kindly missions, I felt that many a single English-woman might do worse than give such a life a trial. To have the privileges and virtues of the nun and be no nun—that is, perhaps, to come as near the secret at any rate as to have the suffrage.

And so by gradual stages we descended to a little waiting-room with a picture by the great Otto Van Veen (Rubens's master, as every Belgian sacristan knows) in it : a picture of Christ in the house of Martha and Mary, with Mary all adoration at His feet, and a table groaning beneath a Flemish profusion of food—hares and fowls and ducks and green stuffs and joints and all the riot that the still-life painters rejoiced in—and poor Martha in the background in despair at ever reducing such chaos to an orderly hospitality without some help from her sister. Velasquez at the National Gallery gives these twain a small yet sturdy servant-maid, but not so Van Veen, Rubens's master. Well, in this room was a table which when we had first entered, half an hour before, was empty, but was now covered with lace ; and by it stood an aged sister inviting us to buy. And buy we certainly should not, had not Sister Lucie Vinken suggested the readiness of the Convent to take a cheque ; and so we went

off with a lace scarf for which I was to send
a cheque made out to a Lady Superior for
twenty-eight francs, waving farewells and calling
out promises to return which I hope will be
fulfilled.

And now for me Sister Lucie Vinken stands
and will stand for Ghent, taking the place of the
galloping Dirck and Joris of Browning's poem,
who for many years, before I set foot there, had
been all of Ghent that I had in mind—their
hoofs beating in my head like a drum whenever
the city was mentioned. But their day is past.
Their noisy onset is over. The word Ghent
henceforward will call forth a serene and prosperous and comfortable cooing lady in black and
white, moving softly from room to room of her
spotless female monastery, all smiles and sympathy and kindness and Rome. Dirck, Joris,
and their sweating steeds have no place here.
Over my new Ghent broods the dove.

LIFE'S LITTLE DIFFICULTIES

The Wedding Present   *o*   *o*   *o*

I

From the Rev. Wilson Large to several of his parishioners, including Lady Fern, Mrs. Harrison Root, Miss Callow, Mrs. Pollard, Sir Anthony Dix, Mr. Horace Sparrow, and Mr. Jack Pyke-Luntin

DEAR ———,—As you no doubt are aware, our friend and neighbour, Lord Clumber, after a period of lonely widowerhood, is about to enter again into the bonds of wedlock, with Miss Birdie Bangle, and it has been thought that, in addition to any little gift which we may individually be sending to him, some general token of our esteem and our desire as a community for his happiness would be timely and welcome. I write to you, as to several others of the leading residents in the neighbourhood, to ask for your co-operation in this little scheme, and for your views as to the shape which the testimonial should take. My own idea is a timepiece, with a suitable inscription on a silver plate beneath the dial.—Believe me, yours cordially, WILSON LARGE

II

Mr. Jack Pyke-Luntin to the Rev. Wilson Large

DEAR LARGE,—If by timepiece you mean clock, I'm on. Of course old Clum has clocks to burn, but wedding presents don't count. It's the thought behind them Put me down for a sovereign, and if I can help you by buying the clock when I go to town next, I will do so gladly. But you must give me all instructions very clearly.—Yours, J. PYKE-LUNTIN

III

Miss Callow to the Rev. Wilson Large

DEAR MR. LARGE,—Your news has made me a new woman. I have been very ill with rheumatism and general depression for so long, but the thought that dear Lord Clumber is again to be made happy has brightened every minute since your letter came. I like the idea of the clock—

how very clever of you ! Such unsuitable presents are often given on these, to me, sacred occasions, such even as spirit flasks and other unpleasantly material things. But of course you, with your views on temperance, would not have permitted anything like that. I enclose a cheque for two guineas.—Yours sincerely and gratefully,

ELLEN CALLOW

IV

Lady Fern to the Rev. Wilson Large

DEAR MR. LARGE,—I am both pained and shocked by the interest you are taking in this unfortunate marriage. When English noblemen marry dancing-girls it is the duty of the clergy to weep rather than organise wedding presents. Your scheme will receive no countenance from me, I remember poor Lady Clumber far too vividly. Any present that I may feel disposed to make will take an admonitory form, or I may possibly send a copy of Lord Avebury's *Pleasures of Life*.—Yours sincerely, ANGELA FERN

V

The Rev. Wilson Large to Lady Fern

MY DEAR LADY FERN,—I was greatly distressed to find that your attitude to Lord Clumber's engagement is so hostile. I fear, in your perhaps natural dislike to see a stranger in the late Lady Clumber's place, you have been betrayed into a slight error. You say a "dancing-girl," but I understand that Miss Bangle spoke quite a number of words in the last play at (I think) the Gaiety Theatre, and by some of the leading critics was very warmly praised for her imaginative treatment of the part. In any case, I doubt if we ought to condemn dancing *quâ* dancing. We have all danced a little in our time—I used, I remember, to be singularly happy in Sir Roger—and Miss Bangle may be a very worthy person in spite of her calling. It is enough for me that Lord Clumber has chosen her.—I am, dear Lady Fern, yours cordially, WILSON LARGE

VI

Sir Anthony Dix to the Rev. Wilson Large

DEAR LARGE,—It's a very good notion, but a clock is too dull. Birdie won't care for a clock at all; not unless she's very different from what she used to be. A motor-coat would be much more in her line, or a tasty fan. I saw some beauties the other day in Bond Street. It's rather a joke for her to catch Clumber; and a good deal of a change for him after the late Lady C. I enclose a cheque for two pounds, anyway.—Yours truly,   ANTHONY DIX

VII

Mrs. Harrison Root to the Rev. Wilson Large

DEAR MR. LARGE,—I cannot find that anyone staying in this Pension knows Miss Bangle's name, although there are several ladies who seem to be ardent playgoers. But perhaps she has only just appeared in London. Mr. Benson, whom I know slightly, is always producing wonderful new Shakspearean actresses, and I imagine Miss Bangle to be one of these. But what an odd name !—Yours sincerely,

GRACE HARRISON ROOT

VIII

Mr. Horace Sparrow to the Rev. Wilson Large

DEAR LARGE,—I think your idea a good one, and I shall be glad to join. But is not a clock a rather unimaginative present ? It always seems to me that insufficient thought is given to such matters. I have put down a few articles which

my wife and I consider more suitable and
original.—Believe me, yours sincerely,

HORACE SPARROW

> Reading Lamp.
> Revolving Bookcase.
> Complete set of Ruskin.
> After-dinner Coffee set.

P.S.—Mrs. Sparrow and myself have derived
more comfort from a breakfast heater than any
other of our very numerous wedding presents.

H. S.

IX

Miss Effie Pollard to the Rev. Wilson Large

DEAR MR. LARGE,—We think it such a charming idea of yours, and shall be delighted to
assist. My mother is in favour of a butter-dish,
but the clock seems to me an admirable thought.
What could be prettier than a reminder such as
this that another hour of happiness has passed,
and that so many friends have good wishes for
the new life! As I tell mother, she can give the
butter-dish independently, if you think that our
one visit to Clumber Towers, on the occasion of
the Missionary Helpers' Union annual fête, a

The Wedding Present

sufficient ground. Meanwhile I enclose a postal order for a pound, and remain yours sincerely,

EFFIE POLLARD

X

The Rev. Wilson Large to Mrs. Harrison Root

DEAR MRS. ROOT,—I am happy to be able to tell you that everything is in train for the wedding present for Lord Clumber. Mr. Pyke-Luntin has very kindly arranged to buy the clock in London, in a shop in Bond Street where I saw them, and to arrange for a suitable inscription. The *Tatler* which you send me is very interesting. Miss Bangle has certainly a very charming face, but it seems to me to border too much on familiarity to call her plain " Birdie " underneath. Lord Clumber can hardly like that. Still, it is not for me to sit in judgment.—Believe me, dear Mrs. Root, yours cordially,

WILSON LARGE

XI

Mr. Jack Pyke-Luntin to the Rev. Wilson Large

DEAR LARGE,—I am sorry to say that the fog yesterday was too much for me altogether, and made it impossible to get to Bond Street. But

Life's Little Difficulties

I managed to struggle as far as the Stores, and I think you will be delighted with what I managed to secure—a real bargain. They had no clocks worth anything, and so I hopped on to this—a first-class Tantalus. It is being engraved to-day, and should reach you to-morrow. I know old Clum will appreciate that, and he's got clocks enough already to tick his head off.—Yours sincerely, J. PYKE-LUNTIN

II

Jane's Eighth or Ninth 〇 〇 〇

Mrs. Wishart to her sister, Mrs. Tylor

DEAR EMILY,—I suppose you have heard that poor Jane is engaged again, and this time it really looks as if it might last. I heard the news from Charlotte, but she says very little. She has not seen him yet. He is a curate named Trevor Singer, and at present is in a church at Hove. It does not sound very grand, but Jane, of course, has her £600 a year, and that should help. She will never give up her horse, I am sure. She is staying at Brighton in a boarding-house, all alone, near a mews. How like her!—Yours, LUCY

Mrs. Tylor to Mrs. Wishart

DEAR LUCY,—What you say about Jane has set us all in a flutter. We have been trying to

133

fix the number of Mr. Singer's predecessors.
Arthur thinks it is seven, but I can only make
six, unless, of course, you count that little architect who came about the new billiard-room. But
surely that was all on one side, although the
same remark might, I suppose, be made about
them all. Well, it is quite time she settled
down, for she must be getting on. Is it thirty-
seven or thirty-eight? A curate at Hove does
not sound very exciting, but Jane always looked
for an amenable man rather than an exciting one.
Just think of that Socialist she used to lead
about when we were all at Overstrand. Which
reminds me that I had forgotten him when I was
counting them up. He makes seven for certain
—with the little architect eight, and with Mr.
Singer nine. I am dying to hear more about it
all.—Yours, EMILY

Mr. Hugh Tylor to Mrs. Tylor

DEAR MOTHER,—Who do you think I saw on
the sea wall yesterday? Jane,—with a very old
parson. She was hanging on his arm just as if
she were his only daughter, and I walked behind
them for ever so far, and then hurried away
before they turned, as I didn't want to meet
them and have the bore of being introduced.

Besides, I didn't want Jane to know I was here, or she would be bothering me to ride out with her beside her old rocking-horse. But I wonder who the parson is and how she got so thick with him. It's a change for her, after her poets and high-art-furniture men.—Your affectionate

HUGH

Mr. Hugh Tylor to Mrs. Tylor

MY DEAR MOTHER,—I cannot answer your questions, I am afraid, as I have not seen the parson again, although I saw Jane on horseback yesterday and was just in time to turn into a by-street. At the "Bedford," where I am, one is rather out of the way of finding out anything about Hove curates, but his name is in the Directory all right. Why don't you try the Clergy List if you want to know more? Or write to Jane yourself. Only if you do, don't say I am at Brighton: I came here for rest. I am quite sure it was an old man—about a hundred, I should say. Certainly not a young and dashing curate.—Your affectionate HUGH

Mrs. Tylor to her niece, Jane Rudstock

MY DEAR JANE,—I have just heard what I hope is a true rumour—that you are engaged.

Life's Little Difficulties

I think you might have told **me** yourself, but no doubt you have had very little time in the midst of your new happiness. Do let me have a line and tell me all about him; what he does, where you will live, what his age is, and so forth.—Your loving aunt, EMILY

Miss Jane Rudstock to Mrs. Tylor

MY DEAR AUNT EMILY,—I am sorry that I did not write to you at once. As a matter of fact I did start a letter to you a day or so ago, but while I was in the midst of it I went for a ride and saw Hugh coming towards me, but the way in which he turned his horse's head up a by-street because he did not want to be bored by meeting me, discouraged me from going on. I am not vindictive, but I am utterly daunted by any suspicion of avoidance in others. As it is, however, unfair to include you in this feeling, I tell you now very readily that the rumour is true. It is a Mr. Singer, a curate at St. Benedict's, Hove, and we hope to be married very soon. He will stay here until he gets a living, which may happen at any moment, as he is on very good terms with both the Bishop and the Archbishop. His age is thirty-four. I could have wished that my husband were older than I, but Trevor won't hear of this. He is totally without relations, and was a very lonely man until I met him—on the Downs above Brighton, where he helped to get a stone out of Tommy's foot.—Your affectionate niece,   JANE

Mrs. Tylor to Mr. Hugh Tylor

MY DEAR HUGH,—The plot thickens. Jane (who, it seems, saw you that day when you were riding, and is hurt by your treatment) tells me that her *fiancé* is only thirty-four. This makes the old clergyman whom you saw her embracing a very mysterious creature. Are you sure it was Jane? It is all very perplexing. You ought to call on the poor girl. She is very unhappy about your behaviour.—Your loving mother.

Mrs. Tylor to Mrs. Wishart

DEAR LUCY,—I have heard from Jane, a nice letter telling me all about Mr. Singer, and how happy she is. One of her delightful, spontaneous, confiding letters. She says that he is thirty-four, but the odd thing is that Hugh, who is at Brighton, saw her hanging on the arm of quite an old clergyman, in public, on the sea wall. As the dear girl says that her *fiancé* has no relations, this is very odd, isn't it? But she always was odd, and made such curious friends.—Yours,

EMILY

Mrs. Rudstock to her daughter, Jane Rudstock

MY DEAREST JANE,—I am so distressed, having heard through your Aunt Lucy a very odd story of your being seen on the Brighton Front in much too friendly intercourse with an old clergyman, just after your engagement to Mr. Singer. My dear child, you must be very careful now that you are engaged. Apart altogether from Mr. Singer's feelings, you must consider us too. It was bad enough to go to Brighton without any chaperon but your eternal horse. Please set my mind at rest by telling me who this old clergyman was. I hope Mr. Singer's grandfather, although I seem to remember that you said he had no relations.—Your fond mother.

From Jane Rudstock to Mrs. Rudstock

MY DEAR MOTHER,—As usual, the whole trouble has come through Aunt Lucy and Aunt Emily. Hugh seems to have been spying about at Brighton and sending home silly letters, although he has not had the friendliness to call on me. There is nothing to explain, except that

Trevor has white hair and from the back might look older than he is. If you were to trust me more it would be better for us all.—Your loving daughter,   JANE

Mrs. Rudstock to her daughter Jane

MY DEAR CHILD,—Your letter fills me with misgivings. Don't say you are marrying an albino. You will be the first Rudstock to do such a thing. Do let me know instantly that his white hair was the result of an illness, or a sudden fright. I cannot bear the thought of my daughter's husband having pink eyes.—Your distressed mother.

Jane Rudstock to Mrs. Rudstock
(Telegram)

Trevor albino right enough. Took double first Oxford. Cousin Lord Lamberhurst. First authority England on Saxon fonts. Amateur champion racquets, 1894. Longs meet you.

                                                  JANE

Mrs. Rudstock to her sister, Mrs. Wishart

DEAR LUCY,—I do wish you would learn a lesson from the past, and not exaggerate simple things. That dreadful trouble over Agnes and the Sunday School treat ought to have taught you something. All the fuss about poor Jane at Brighton is due to the simple fact that Mr. Singer, to whom she is engaged, has prematurely white hair—is, in fact, an albino. Why he should not be I cannot see. In fact, I think albinos quite attractive, and they are notoriously cleverer than other people. He is a dear good fellow, a great scholar and athlete, and the cousin of Lord Lamberhurst, and we are all going to be very fond of him. Please write Jane a nice letter.—Yours,

CHARLOTTE

Mrs. Wishart to Mrs. Tylor

DEAR EMILY,—It is so funny I can hardly hold the pen. Jane's choice is an albino, and that accounts for the white hair. Charlotte is trying to brave it out and pretend that she could not love any son-in-law who had not white hair and pink eyes, but of course she is mortified to death at the humiliation of it. Poor Jane! How they can allow an albino to take orders I can't think, especially when the Church is threatened on all sides as it now is; but there you are. I wish you had sent on Jane's confiding, spontaneous letter about her freak, but I suppose you had your reasons for not doing so.—Yours,

LUCY

III

The Chauffeur ◦ ◦ ◦ ◦ ◦

i

Mrs. Adrian Armyne to her sister
(Extract)

WE have found a most delightful chauffeur, a
Frenchman named Achille Le Bon, who speaks
English perfectly, although with a fascinating
accent, and is altogether most friendly and
useful. He is continually doing little things
for me, and it is nice too to have someone to talk
French with. Adrian's conversational French
has always been very rusty. You remember how
in that little shop at Avignon in 1887 he said
" Quel dommage ? " for *" What is the price ? "*

II

Mr. Adrian Armyne to the Conservative Agent at
Wilchester

Mr. Adrian Armyne presents his compliments
to Mr. Bashford, and greatly regrets what must

look very like a slight in his absence from the chair at last night's meeting, but circumstances over which he had no control caused him to miss the way in his motor-car and afterwards to break down at a spot where it was impossible to get any other vehicle. Mr. Armyne cannot too emphatically express his regret at the occurrence, and his hope that trust in his good faith as a worker in the cause of Fiscal Reform may not be permanently shattered.

III

Sir Vernon Boyce to Mr. Armyne

DEAR ARMYNE,—I think you ought to know that I came across your Frenchman with a gun in the Lower Spinney this morning, evidently intending to get what he could. He explained to me that he distinctly understood you to say that he was at liberty to shoot there. How such a misunderstanding can have arisen I cannot guess, but he is now clearly informed as to divisions of land and other matters which apparently are different in France. It is all right, but I think you ought to keep an eye on him.—Yours sincerely,

VERNON BOYCE

The Chauffeur

IV

Mrs. Armyne to her sister
(Extract)

Achille is certainly very useful, although his mercurial French nature makes him a little too careless about time, and once or twice he has been nowhere to be found at important junctures. For instance, we completely missed Lord Tancaster's wedding the other day. Not that that mattered very much, especially as we had sent a silver inkstand, but Adrian is rather annoyed. Achille plays the mandoline charmingly (we hear him at night in the servants' hall), and he has been teaching me *repoussé* work.

V

Mrs. Armyne to Mrs. Jack Lyon

DEAR MRS. LYON,—My husband and myself are deeply distressed to have put out your table last evening, but it was one of those accidents that occur now and then, and which there is no foreseeing or remedying. The fact is that we were all ready to go and had ordered the car, when it transpired that Achille, our chauffeur, had been called to London by telegram, and had left in so great a hurry that he had no time to warn us.

By the time we could have sent to the village and got a carriage your dinner would have been over, and so we decided not to go at all. Achille has not yet returned, which makes us fear that the poor fellow, who has relatives in Soho, may have found real trouble.—Yours sincerely,

EMILY ARMYNE

VI

Mr. Armyne to Achille Le Bon

DEAR ACHILLE,—I am very sorry to have to tell you that it has been made necessary for us to ask you to go. This is not on account of any dissatisfaction that we have with you, but merely that Mrs. Armyne has heard of the son of an old housekeeper of her father's who wishes for a post as chauffeur, and she feels it only right that he should be given a trial. You will, I am sure, see how the case stands. Perhaps we had better say that a month's notice begins from to-day, but you may leave as much earlier as you like. I shall, of course, be only too pleased to do all I can to find you another situation. I should have told you this in person, but had to go to town, and now write because I think it would be wrong not to let you have as early an intimation of Mrs. Armyne's decision as possible.—I am, yours faithfully,

ADRIAN ARMYNE

The Chauffeur

VII

Mr. Armyne to Achille Le Bon
(By hand)

DEAR ACHILLE,—I am afraid that a letter which was posted to you from London when I was last there, a month ago, cannot have reached you. Letters are sometimes lost, and this must be one of them. In it I had to inform you that Mrs. Armyne, having made arrangements for an English chauffeur who has claims on her consideration (being the son of an old housekeeper of her father's, who was in his service for many years, and quite one of the family), it was made necessary for us, much against our will, for we esteem you very highly, to ask you to go. As that letter miscarried, I must now repeat the month's notice that I then was forced to give, and the permission for you to leave at any time within the month if you like.—I am, yours faithfully,

ADRIAN ARMYNE

VIII

Mr. Armyne to his nephew, Sidney Burnet
(Extract)

There seems to be nothing for it but to sell our car. This is a great blow to us, but we cannot go on as we are, apparently owning a car but in reality being owned by a chauffeur.

IX

Sidney Burnet to Mr. Armyne

DEAR UNCLE,—Don't sell the car. The thing to do is to pretend to sell it, get rid of your Napoleon, and then have it back. Why not say I have bought it? I will come over one day soon and drive it home. Say Thursday morning.—Your affectionate nephew,   SIDNEY

X

Mr. Armyne to Mr. Sidney Burnet

MY DEAR SIDNEY,—Your plan seems to me to be ingenious, but your aunt is opposed to it. She says that Achille might find it out. Suppose, for example, he came back for something he had forgotten and saw the car in the coach-house again! What should we do? Another objection is that poor Job is ill, and Achille remarked to me the other day that before he took to engineering he was a gardener. From what I know of him, this means that unless Job gets better, Achille — if

146

your plan is carried through—will ask to be retained in Job's place, and this will mean that we shall never see asparagus or strawberries again. Don't you think that we might go to town, and you could ride over to "Highfield" and give Achille notice yourself for me? We will go to town to-morrow, and you might see Achille on Monday.—Your affectionate uncle.

XI

Sidney Burnet to Mr. Armyne

DEAR UNCLE,—I went over and sacked Achille to-day as arranged, but he replied that he could take notice only from you; and that from what Aunt Emily had said to him just before you went away he is sure there has been some mistake. As to notice from you, I'm afraid the beggar's right. He seems to have taken advantage of your absence to build a really rather clever pergola leading from Aunt Emily's sitting-room to the rose walk, as a surprise for Mrs. Armyne, he said. He has also re-painted all your bookshelves and mended that pair of library steps. With the despatch of this bulletin I retire from the position of discharger of Frenchmen.—Your affectionate nephew, SIDNEY

Life's Little Difficulties

XII

Mrs. Jack Lyon to a friend a few months later
(Extract)

You remember the Armynes? In despair at ever getting rid of their chauffeur, who certainly led them a fearful dance, although he was rather a dear creature, the poor things let their house for a year and decided to travel. I have just heard from Bella, from Florence, that she met them toiling up the hill to Fiesole the other day, and behind them, carrying Mrs. Armyne's easel, was—who do you think? The chauffeur!

The Dedication ✑ ✑ ✑ ✑ ✑

I

Mr. Launcelot Wyke Pilling, of "The Dryads,"
Worthing, to Dr. W. Porter Roddy, Mereham,
Norfolk

DEAR DR. RODDY,—I am just collecting together
in one volume all my fugitive poetry of the past
nine years, since the publication of my *Death of
Ham, and other Poems,* and it would give me great
pleasure to dedicate the book to you, not only as
some recognition of your industry as an antiquary,
but also as an acknowledgment of the great skill
which you displayed during my long and very severe
illness last summer, from which I am now happily
recovered, save for an increased tendency to take
cold.—Believe me, dear Doctor, yours very truly,

LAUNCELOT WYKE PILLING

II

Dr. Roddy to Mr. Pilling

MY DEAR MR. PILLING,—Your letter, with its flattering offer, does me too much honour. The archæologist quickly gets into the habit of not looking for recognition or reward. Perhaps, as antiquity has worked for him, it is only right that he should work for posterity. Hence, although such *coups* as I may have brought off in the fields of archæology and folk-lore have been commemorated in the local press and in the minutes of our Society, the wider world knows almost nothing of me. The dedication page of your volume will be the first intimation of my name and career to a large portion of the English-speaking community. I thank you very heartily for your courtesy. Perhaps you will let me have a notion of the form which the dedication will take. As for your tendency to catch cold, of which I am very sorry to hear, I would recommend the adoption of an abdominal belt, often a sure precautionary measure.—Believe me, my dear Sir, yours very truly,

W. PORTER RODDY

The Dedication

III

Mr. Pilling to Dr. Roddy

DEAR DR. RODDY,—It gratifies me extremely to find that you will allow your name to honour my poor bantling. The dedication will run thus :—

To W. PORTER RODDY, M.D.

the modern Galen to whom the author owes his life, recently jeopardised on a visit to the East Coast by a severe attack of rheumatoid arthritis, and the modern Old-buck to whose imaginative labour and indefatigable researches into the storied past the townspeople of Mereham and the in-habitants of East Norfolk generally owe so much, this volume is, with respect and admiration, dedicated.

I think that that expresses the case very clearly and, if I may say so, with a pleasant allu-siveness, and I feel sure that you will agree with me. I am ordering an abdominal belt.—Believe me, dear Doctor, yours very truly,

LAUNCELOT WYKE PILLING

P.S.—I re-open this to say that I have suddenly become the victim of a most curious and,

to me, alarming singing in the ears, so loud that I
can hardly hear anything that is going on.

L. W. P.

IV

Dr. Roddy to Mr. Pilling

DEAR MR. PILLING,—The wording of the dedication is very flattering, and I am so much
honoured by it that I hesitate to utter a syllable
of criticism; but since you have been so kind I
am emboldened to suggest that a more suitable
predecessor than *Oldbuck* might be found.   For
two reasons: (1) he was a character not in real
life but in fiction, in a novel by Sir Walter Scott,
and Galen being a real man I would suggest,
with all deference, that whatever antiquary you
choose should be real too; and (2) if by any
typographical disaster, such as are, unhappily,
only too frequent in our local press, a space were
to intervene between the first and second syllables
of his name, the reference to me would become
instantly not respectful as you so kindly desire,
but grotesque.   I trust I make myself clear.   I
would suggest the substitute of some such name
as Aubrey or Leland.

The singing in the ears has probably passed
away by this time; but if it has not I should

take a tonic. Weston's Syrup might be useful, and it is easily obtained of any chemist.—Believe me, yours very truly,   W. PORTER RODDY

▼

Mr. Pilling to Dr. Roddy

DEAR DR. RODDY,—I am sorry that you take exception to my dedication, which was, I assure you, not idly thrown off, but represents the work of some hours of thought. Your objection to *Oldbuck* illustrates once again the impossibility of reconciling science with poetry. I, a poet, wishing my dedication to be in keeping with my book, choose deliberately a figure of the imagination from the greatest of all modern novelists (whom you do not, I fear, sufficiently esteem). You, being a man of science, require me to substitute the name of some fusty old bookworm and tombstone-scraper from real life. Few people give way to criticism so readily as I, but in this case I really must be firm.

The singing in the head, which you treat so lightly, still continues to cause me the gravest concern. I have taken two doses of the syrup without any relief.—Believe me, yours truly,

LAUNCELOT WYKE PILLING

Life's Little Difficulties

VI

Dr. Roddy to Mr. Pilling

DEAR MR. PILLING,—I am sorry that we cannot
see eye to eye in this matter. I have taken the
liberty of submitting your dedication to several
of my friends, including the Vicar, an exception-
ally gifted man, and the Curator of the Museum,
whose memoir on bees is a standard work, and
all agree with me that a suggestion of not pre-
cisely frivolity but want of the highest seriousness
is imparted by the reference to *Jonathan Oldbuck*.
The Vicar is also of opinion that it is, perhaps,
understating the case to limit my reputation, as
you do, to East Norfolk, since I have several
times contributed to *Notes and Queries*. I have,
however, done with criticism, and beg to repeat
my thanks to you for your kindness.

A tonic requires time to do its work. Two
doses could not effect any material improvement.
The singing is probably over by now.—Believe
me, yours very truly,   W. PORTER RODDY

VII

Mr. Pilling to Dr. Roddy

DEAR DR. RODDY,—I am horrified to learn that
you have committed the solecism—the unpardon-

able solecism — of showing my dedication to strangers. Were you more conversant with the laws, written or unwritten, of authorship, you would know that this is never done : that everything is avoided that can take the fine edge of novelty from a new book. The incident has completely disheartened me, and I am quite incapable of attending any further to the dedication.

To add to it all, the singing in my ears increases.—Believe me, yours faithfully,

LAUNCELOT WYKE PILLING

VIII

Dr. Roddy to Mr. Pilling

DEAR MR. PILLING,—I am extremely sorry ; but my friends read the dedication in strictest confidence, and I was quite unaware that I was offending. Perhaps the matter had better drop altogether. You will have, I am sure, no difficulty in finding a worthier and less critical object to whom to offer your volume.—Believe me, yours very truly,

W. PORTER RODDY

Life's Little Difficulties

IX

Mr. Pilling to the Bishop of Caster

My Lord,—I am just collecting together in one volume all my fugitive poetry of the past nine years,—since, in fact, the publication of my *Death of Ham, and other Poems,*—and it would give me great pleasure and confer a high distinction upon the book, if I might be permitted to dedicate it to you, not only to mark your interest in poetry, but also from personal gratitude for benefits received from your Lenten sermons last year, which I attended with my wife, and which we still vividly remember.—Believe me, my Lord, your obedient servant,

Launcelot Wyke Pilling

X

The Rev. Cyril Blood (Private Secretary to the Bishop of Caster) to Mr. Pilling

Dear Sir,—I am instructed by the Bishop to say that he will be pleased to accept the dedication to which you refer; but that if you propose to make it a lengthy one he must insist on seeing a proof.—I am, yours faithfully,

Cyril Blood

V

The Appointment ∽ ∽ ∽ ∽

I

Mr. Adrian Spilling, of the Education Office, to
Miss Meta Bland

(By hand. " Wait reply ")

MY DEAR GIRL,—What has happened? I
waited for you from five minutes to three until
twenty past four, when I had to go in order
to show up in Whitehall for a little while.
Where can you have been? It is not as if
I had so much time to spare that it can be
frittered away like this. Surely I wrote clearly
enough—" Under the clock, Victoria, at three."
I distinctly remember writing these words.
Please let me have a line at any rate to say
you are all right.—Yours always,

A.

Life's Little Difficulties

II

Miss Meta Bland to Mr. Adrian Spilling

(By hand. " Wait reply ")

MY DEAR ADRIAN,—Do send me a word to say you are well, and that it was only some horrid office business that kept you. I am so nervous about you. I waited as you told me under the clock at Victoria, from five minutes past three (I could not possibly get there before) until four, and then I gave it up and went to Mrs. Legge's to tea, as I was compelled to do. Unless you had come and gone before I got there, I cannot have missed you, for I watched everybody that entered the station. These broken appointments are terribly wearing. I am tired out this evening, and quite unfit to dine at the Sergisons, where they always talk about Velasquez and show you sprigs of the true poet's laurel.—Ever yours,

M.

Miss Meta Bland to Mr. Adrian Spilling

(By hand. Answer to No. 1)

DEAR ADRIAN,—I haven't the slightest idea what your letter means. I repeat that I waited under the clock at Victoria from five minutes past three until four.   If you also were there you were invisible.   I am relieved to find you are all right.—Yours,   M.

IV

Mr. Adrian Spilling to Miss Meta Bland

(By hand.   Answer to No. 2)

DEAR META,—It is inexplicable to me.   I was certainly there, and as certainly you were not; and another afternoon has been lost.   These things I simply cannot view with composure. Life is too short.   I will let you know about Thursday as soon as I can, but my Chief seems to be inclined to resent my long absence to day, and I shall have to be a little careful.—Yours,   A.

P.S.—It has just occurred to me that you may have been waiting at the London and Brighton part of the station.   That, of course, would explain it, although how you could imagine me to mean that I cannot think.

V

Miss Meta Bland to Mr. Adrian Spilling

DEAR ADRIAN,—I have only just learned that there are two stations at Victoria.   Considering how often I have been to Brighton lately, you surely might have been more explicit and said quite plainly that it was the other that you meant. It is all very foolish and disappointing. I should like to forget it.—Yours,   M.

VI

Mr. Adrian Spilling to Miss Meta Bland

DEAR META,—I should like to forget it too; but what you say simply bowls me out. I always looked upon you as one of the few women who have any intelligence. How you can say you did not know there was another Victoria passes my knowledge, when it was from there that we went on that awful visit to your aunt at Faversham. However, I shall know better next time.—Yours,   A.

VII

Miss Meta Bland to Mr. Adrian Spilling

DEAR ADRIAN,—I thought we went to Faversham from Charing Cross; but anyway I don't see why you are so bitter about poor Aunt Adelaide. I am sure she was very kind to you, and even let you smoke in the house, which no one was ever allowed to do before. It seems to me that since

you knew all about there being two Victoria
Stations you might have walked over to the
other one to see if I was there.—Yours,

M.

VIII

Mr. Adrian Spilling to Miss Meta Bland

DEAR META,—I don't understand you at all
about your aunt. All the time we were there
you were scheming to be out of doors, and I still
remember your sigh of relief when the train
started on the Monday morning; but now you
take a directly opposite view. I suppose women
are like this. As to coming over to the Brighton
side to see if you were there, I never dreamed
you could be so foolish as to make the mistake,
and besides, if I had left my post I might have
missed you. But do let us drop this wretched
subject.

I am very sorry to say that I can't possibly
take you to hear Kreisler on Friday as we had
planned. My Chief has asked me to dinner, and
it amounts to a command. But I could come
afterwards and take you home.—Yours,

A.

Life's Little Difficulties

IX

Miss Meta Bland to Mr. Adrian Spilling

DEAR ADRIAN,—It doesn't in the least matter
about Kreisler, as Mr. Cumnor-Hall, who was
here this evening when your note came, is going
to take us. Please don't trouble to leave your
party in order to fetch me home, as Mr.
Cumnor-Hall has asked us to have supper afterwards. He is always so generous about things
like that.—Yours,   M.

Mr. Adrian Spilling to Miss Meta Bland

DEAR META,—Of course you must do as you
wish about Cumnor-Hall. I shall certainly not
come to fetch you, as he is not the kind of man
that I care about. Your sneer about my want
of generosity is the cruellest thing I ever remember anyone saying to me. When one has
only £300 a year in a Government office, and a
very small private income, supper parties at the
Savoy are not easy things. If you want
luxuries like that it is a pity you ever made
me love you.—Yours,   A

The Appointment

Miss Meta Bland to Mr. Adrian Spilling

DEAR ADRIAN,—You are most unkind and unfair. You know I did not mean to suggest that you were ungenerous. I think of you as the most generous man I know. And you ought to know that the last thing I should ever do would be to sneer at you. I don't sneer at anyone, least of all at you. But that horrid Victoria Station affair seems to have made us both ready to misunderstand each other. Do let us have all Saturday afternoon somewhere and forget this stupid, bad-tempered week.—Ever yours,   M.

XII

Mr. Adrian Spilling to Miss Meta Bland

(*By hand*)

MY DARLING META,—We will go to Kew on Saturday afternoon. I will come for you at half-past two. I hope you will think this little piece of enamel rather sweet. I do.—Yours always,

A.

VI

The Testimonial ⟁ ⟁ ⟁ ⟁

I

*Jabez Copley, of Copley's Stores, to the leading
residents of Great Burley and neighbourhood*

(CYCLOSTYLE)

THE MISSENDEN TESTIMONIAL FUND

DEAR SIR (or MADAM),—I have the honour to
inform you that our worthy Stationmaster Mr.
Missenden, having received promotion, is leaving
us very shortly for a higher sphere of activity, and
some of his friends met together last night at the
" King's Arms " to confer as to a testimonial to
be presented to him. Greatly to my surprise, I
was asked to undertake the duties of hon.
secretary and hon. treasurer, and it is in these
capacities that I take the liberty of addressing
you. The meeting decided to open a subscrip-

tion list for Mr. Missenden in the town and neighbourhood, and to present him with the proceeds and with an illuminated address.

The following is the address that was drawn up —I may say by myself:—

Presented to

JAMES HENRY MISSENDEN

BY THE GENTRY AND INHABITANTS OF GREAT BURLEY

on the occasion of his departure from that Town, on the completion of nearly Eight Years of honourable service as Station Master, to take up a post of increased responsibility at Clapham Junction — as a mark of their appreciation of his Courtesy and Efficiency during his period of office at Great Burley Terminus.

This address will be engrossed in several colours and in gold, with appropriate borders and scroll-work (as in the illuminated texts in our bedrooms) by Miss Millie Feathers, at the school, who is very clever and artistic with her hands, and presented to Mr. Missenden, with the purse, at the "King's Arms" on a suitable evening.—Awaiting your reply, I am, dear Sir (or Madam), yours obediently,   JABEZ COPLEY

Hon. Sec. and Treasurer of the
Missenden Testimonial Fund

Life's Little Difficulties

Added, in Mr. Copley's own hand, to a few of the letters

P.S.—It is not my wish to intrude business, but I feel it would be wrong not to take this opportunity of informing you that I have just received a particularly advantageous line of preserved fruits, which I can do at extraordinarily low terms.   No time should be lost in ordering.

II

Miss Mill to Mr. Jabez Copley

DEAR MR. COPLEY,—I had no idea that the Stationmaster was going.   How interesting to find that his name is Missenden!   It was the name of my mother's favourite cook.   She came, I think from Esher, or it may have been Exeter. It is odd how long one may live without knowing the name of one's Stationmaster, although my niece tells me it has to be painted up somewhere, like a licensed victualler's.   I think I should like to try a box of the preserved fruit if it is really nice.—Yours truly,

LYDIA MILL

The Testimonial

Sir Charles Transom's Secretary to Mr. Jabez Copley

DEAR SIR,—Sir Charles Transom directs me to present his compliments and to express his regret that he must decline to lend his support to the testimonial to the Great Burley Stationmaster. Sir Charles dislikes to see this kind of premium put upon duty, nor can he forget the want of sympathetic zeal and alacrity displayed by the Stationmaster in the autumn of 1898 in the matter of a lost portmanteau containing the manuscript of Sir Charles' monograph on the Transom family.—Believe me, yours faithfully,

VINCENT A. LINCOLN

The Vicar of Great Burley to Mr. Jabez Copley

DEAR MR. COPLEY,—I am afraid I cannot associate myself very cordially with the terms of your testimonial to Mr. Missenden. Eight years is a very short period to signalise in this way, and I do not care for the part played by the "King's Arms." I am sorry to have to take this line; but we must act as we believe. I should be seriously vexed if you got up a testimonial for me after so short a term of work.—I am, yours sincerely,

REGINALD LOWTHER

v

Mr. Jabez Copley to the Vicar of Great Burley

REVEREND SIR,—I regret that you cannot give your valuable and esteemed support to the testimonial to Mr. Missenden, but I respect your motives. I should like to say in reply to your suggestion about a testimonial to yourself and my connection with it, that I should never, I hope, so far presume as to take the leading part in a movement of this kind for a gentleman like yourself. My rule in life is that station should keep to station, and I trust I shall never be so foolish as to depart from it. But although I should not presume to take a leading part in your testimonial, as you kindly suggest, I should, however, contribute to it with a whole heart.—Believe me, yours obediently,

JABEZ COPLEY
Hon. Sec. and Treasurer of the
Missenden Testimonial Fund

The Testimonial

VI

Mr. Aylmer Penistone to Mr. Jabez Copley

DEAR MR. COPLEY,—I do not quite feel disposed to give anything to Missenden. You should draw up a different testimonial for those of us who travel third-class, omitting the word "courtesy."—I am, yours faithfully,

AYLMER PENISTONE

VII

Mrs. Lyon Mounteney to Mr. Jabez Copley

Mrs. Mounteney is very pleased to see, from Mr. Copley's letter, that a spirit of frendliness and comradeship is abroad in Great Burley. Would that all English towns had the same generous feelings! Not having used the railway for several years, owing to her poor health, Mrs. Mounteney does not feel that she could with propriety identify herself with so personal a testimonial, but she wishes it every success. Mrs. Mounteney does not care for preserved fruit.

VIII

Mr. Murray Collier, L.R.C.P., to Mr. Jabez Copley

DEAR MR. COPLEY,—A difficulty with regard to the boys' boxes, which occurs regularly at the

end of each term, and which brings out Mr.
Missenden's native churlishness like a rash, makes
it impossible for me to support your appeal.
After what I have had to say and write to the
Stationmaster it would seem pure pusillanimity
to give him money and praise. May I, however,
suggest the emendation of one small oversight
in your otherwise tasteful address? By no
possible means can our little wayside station be
described as a "terminus," which is a Latin
word signifying the end, as I fancy your son
Harold (whom we all find a very promising and
attractive boy) would be able to tell you.—I am,
yours sincerely, MURRAY COLLIER

IX

*Mr. Jabez Copley to the leading residents of Great
Burley and Neighbourhood*

(CYCLOSTYLE)

THE MISSENDEN TESTIMONIAL FUND

DEAR SIR (or MADAM),—I beg to inform you
that at an influential and representative meeting
held last evening at the "King's Arms," it was
decided with much regret not to take any further
steps with regard to the testimonial to Mr.
Missenden, and to return to the several donors

the £4, 17s. 6d. which the united efforts of myself and two of my assistants have been able to collect in the past month, minus an amount of one guinea to Miss Millie Feathers for work already done on the illuminated address, which cannot, we fear, owing to the peculiar nature of the wording and its reference to Clapham Junction, be adapted to suit any other person.

If anything is now done to indicate to Mr. Missenden that Great Burley appreciates his services, which is very doubtful, it will be done by a few personal friends, at the "King's Arms." I may say here that I have decided under no conditions to ever again undertake the duties of Secretary or Treasurer of a Testimonial, whether hon. or even well paid.—Believe me, dear Sir (or Madam), yours obediently,

JABEZ COPLEY

P.S.—As I am now laying down for ever the pen of the testimonial promoter, I may return to my true vocation as a purveyor of high-class provisions by saying that I have received this morning a consignment of sardines of a new and reliable brand, which I can do at 6½d. the box.

VII

The Box ⟋ ⟋ ⟋ ⟋ ⟋

I

Mrs. Smythe-Smith to Mrs. Clisby

DEAR MRS. CLISBY,—I wonder if you would care to use the enclosed box for the Mausoleum Theatre on Thursday week. We intended to go ourselves, but my husband finds that he will have to travel North that day in connection with an important case.—With kind regards, I am, yours truly, RUTH SMYTHE-SMITH

II

Mrs. Clisby to Mrs. Henderson

MY DEAR MRS. HENDERSON,—Would you and Mr. Henderson care to join us at the Mausoleum on Thursday week? We have a box for that night, and should be so glad if you would look

in. Just ask for Mrs. Clisby's box.—With kind
regards, I am, yours sincerely,

MABEL CLISBY

III

Mrs. Clisby to her sister, Mrs. Thoms

MY DEAR SOPHY,—Our friends the Smythe-
Smiths (he is the barrister) have sent us a box,
which they are unfortunately prevented from
using, for the Mausoleum on Thursday week.
Will you and Henry join us? We are also
asking some nice people we met at Matlock in
the summer—the Hendersons. Mr. Henderson
is in an important position at Lloyd's, and his
wife, who is very charming, is a cousin of Sir
Wilson Arkstone, who made the Corve Tunnel.
—Your loving   M.

IV

Mrs. Thoms to Mrs. Clisby

DEAR MABEL,—We shall love to come to the
theatre with you. But Aggie insists on coming
too, and bringing Bertie Rawler with her. I am
sure you won't mind, she has so few pleasures,
and Bertie, who is always so considerate, can

stand at the back if we are at all crowded. He is quite like one of ourselves already, and I have no hesitation in asking him to do all kinds of little things like this. If only he could get some permanent and lucrative employment, we should be so happy. At present he is an agent for a new kind of combined fountain pen and office ruler, which he is trying very hard to introduce into the City, but without much success, I am afraid.—Your loving   S.

v

Mrs. Clisby to Mrs. Thoms

MY DEAR SOPHY,—I am very sorry to have to disappoint you, but really I don't see how we can manage Mr. Rawler on Thursday night. I am sure that eight will be plenty, and Frank, who is so impetuous, entirely without my knowledge has asked a Mr. Flack, an American over here on business, to whom he wishes to show some kindness, to join us. So that if Aggie comes, and I am so sorry to have forgotten to mention the dear girl when I wrote first, we shall be eight—four couples—without Mr. Rawler.—Your loving   M

The Box

Mrs. Thoms to Mrs. Clisby

DEAR MABEL,—It does not matter about Bertie.
We have arranged that he shall go to the Upper
Circle and come and see us between the acts.
Do tell me a little more about Mr. Flack. What
is his business? Some Americans can be very
attractive. I suppose he has left his wife and
family in America?—Your loving   S.

VII

Mrs. Clisby to Mrs. Thoms

MY DEAR SOPHY,—If Mr. Rawler is coming to
see us between the acts I think he ought to dress.
Couldn't he get a seat in the Dress Circle?—Your
loving   M.

VIII

Mrs. Thoms to Mrs. Clisby

DEAR MABEL,—Of course Bertie will dress.
Going to the theatre is no novelty for him. He
was at school with two of Wilson Barrett's sons.
You do not answer my question about Mr. Flack.
I always like to know in advance something about
the people I am going to meet.—Your loving
                                                S.

Life's Little Difficulties

IX

Mrs. Clisby to Mrs. Thoms

(*By hand*)

MY VERY DEAR SOPHY,—A most unfortunate thing has happened. Chancing to be in the neighbourhood this morning, Frank looked in at the theatre just to see in the plan where our box was, and perhaps mention to one of the officials that you and the Hendersons would be asking for it in the evening. To his horror he found that it was a top box, capable of holding four persons at the most, two of whom could not see the stage except by leaning over very uncomfortably. It is unpardonable of Mrs. Smythe-Smith not to have told me. The question now is, What shall we do? After thinking it over very carefully, I wonder if you would mind postponing your visit to the theatre for a while until there is a better play—the papers seem to think very little of the thing now on—and bringing Mr. Rawler to dinner on Sunday at half-past one. It is so very difficult for me to put off the Hendersons. I am so sorry to have to ask you to be so unselfish, but blood is thicker than water, isn't it?—Your loving   M.

P.S.—Mr. Flack seems to be a man of means.

He is connected with a new patent, and we are very glad to be able to do something to make his time in London less lonely. Frank in putting him off will make some other arrangement.

x

Mrs. Thoms to Mrs. Clisby

(By hand)

DEAR MABEL,—What a pity you did not find out how many the box would hold! I had a feeling, as I mentioned to Henry quite at the first, that you were asking too many. Of course we should like to come to dinner on Sunday, and will do so with pleasure; but I can't help thinking that the best thing to do now is for you to telegraph to the Hendersons that you are ill and have given the box away, and then to take just Aggie and Mr. Flack. The poor girl badly needs a little excitement, and it would be very unfortunate if Frank had to be discourteous to this young American.—Your loving   S.

XI

Mrs. Clisby to Mrs. Thoms

(By hand)

DEAR SOPHY,—Before your reply came I had written to the Hendersons putting them off, but a telegram came from them almost immediately after to say that they would not be able to come, as Mrs. H. has influenza. I am so vexed that I wrote. By all means let Aggie come and meet Mr. Flack. Did I tell you he is quite elderly? His wife came to England with him, but has gone to Stratford-on-Avon and Salisbury for a few days.—Your loving   M.

XII

Mrs. Thoms to Mrs. Clisby

(*By hand*)

DEAR MABEL,—Aggie cannot come after all, as Bertie's brother is taking them to the Hippodrome. We will be punctual on Sunday, and very likely shall bring Bertie's brother with us. I am sure you won't mind.—Your loving   S.

VIII

The Doctor's Visit ✿   ✿   ✿   ✿

I

Mrs. Baring-Rayne to Dr. Tunks

(By hand)

MY DEAR DOCTOR,—It would be a *great solace and satisfaction* to me if you would in future kindly change your hour of call from half-past eleven to *half-past ten* every morning.—Yours sincerely,   EDITHA BARING-RAYNE

Oct. 27

II

Dr. Tunks to Mrs. Baring-Rayne

(By hand)

MY DEAR MRS. BARING-RAYNE, — Your very reasonable request puts me, I regret to say, in a position of some delicacy. It has long been my habit to call on Miss Cann at half-past ten, and Col. Stubbs at eleven, reaching you at 11.30. Both these patients have been in my care for some years, and I feel sure that you will see at once on reading this how difficult it would be for me suddenly to change a custom of such long standing.—Believe me, yours sincerely,

WILBRAHAM TUNKS

Oct. 27

III

Mrs. Baring-Rayne to Dr. Tunks

(*By hand*)

DEAR DOCTOR,—I am sorry to say that I cannot share your view. Health, as I have often heard you say, is the *most important thing* there is, and I am convinced that my health would *in every way* benefit if I could begin the day *earlier.* I have been reading a very interesting pamphlet on the subject of early rising, and am convinced that to wait for you until half-past eleven, when so much of *the sweetest and freshest part of the day* is over, is *a great mistake.* Of course when I wrote I assumed that you have been sincere in your interest in my health, and would immediately comply with so *simple a request.* But life is *one long disillusionment.*—Yours sadly,

EDITHA BARING-RAYNE

Oct. 27

IV

Dr. Tunks to Miss Cann

(*By hand*)

MY DEAR MISS CANN,—I have been thinking lately a good deal about your new pains, and I cannot help feeling that it would be better if you were to rest longer in the morning before being disturbed. I therefore propose in future to call at 11.30 instead of 10.30, at any rate for a sufficient time to test the accuracy of this theory.—Believe me, yours sincerely,

WILBRAHAM TUNKS

Oct. 27

V

Miss Cann to Dr. Wilbraham Tunk.

(*By hand*)

MY DEAR DOCTOR,—Your letter has so shaken me that I fear the worst. It is quite impossible for me, as I thought you knew, to remain in bed so long. I know of nothing so depressing as

181

these long, solitary morning hours.   Please never refer again to the subject, and believe me, yours sincerely,   VICTORIA CANN

P.S.—Sometimes I think it would be better for all of us if I gave up the struggle altogether.
V. C.

VI

Dr. Tunks to Mrs. Baring-Rayne

(*By hand*)

MY DEAR MRS. BARING-RAYNE,—It grieves me exceedingly to have to say so, but I see no possible way of meeting you in your request as to change of visiting hours.   Nor can I agree with the author of your pamphlet that it would be well for you to begin the strain and worry of the day a minute earlier than you now do.   You must, however, do as you think fit.   As you know, I am the last person to wish to impose any tyrannical system upon my patients and friends. I should also say that Miss Cann, much as I should like to effect an interchange of hours, is not, I consider, in a sufficiently robust state to bear it.—Believe me, yours sincerely,

WILBRAHAM TUNKS

Oct. 27

The Doctor's Visit

Mrs. Baring-Rayne to Dr. Tunks

(By hand)

DEAR DOCTOR,—You of course know best, but from the number of tradesmen's carts that draw up at Miss Cann's door it is clear that *she* at any rate has an *appetite*. Whereas I, *as you know*, have eaten *nothing for years*. But it is evident that there is more in this distressing business than *meets the eye*, and I shall therefore take my own steps to protect my health. Do not therefore call to-morrow at all.—Yours truly,

EDITHA BARING-RAYNE

Oct. 27

VIII

Mrs. Baring-Rayne to Mr. Llewellyn Boakes, M.R.C.S.

(By hand)

Mrs. Baring-Rayne presents her compliments to Mr. Llewellyn Boakes, and would be glad if he would call to see her to-morrow morning at half-past ten.

Oct. 27

Life's Little Difficulties

IX

Mr. Boakes to Mrs. Baring-Rayne

(*By hand*)

Mr. Llewellyn Boakes will have great pleasure in calling upon Mrs. Baring-Rayne to-morrow morning. He regrets, however, that owing to appointments with other patients he will be unable to reach Mrs. Baring-Rayne at the hour she names, but he will be at her house certainly not later than eleven-thirty.

Oct. 27

X

Extract from a letter from Mrs. Baring-Rayné to her Sister-in-law

If you ask why my letter is so dismal, it is because I have lost my regular medical attendant. It is a long story, but owing to a *very curious line of conduct* which he chose to take up, we . .

Nov. 2

XI

Mrs. Baring-Rayne to Mr. Boakes

(*By hand*)

Dear Mr. Boakes,—I have been feeling of late so *much worse—much worse* than I have told you, for it is not right to burden others with *all our troubles*—that on the advice of a little pamphlet I have decided on a complete change of routine, the leading principle of which is *total avoidance of all vegetable food.* Although I do not as a rule put any faith in such literature, yet I am convinced that the writer of the pamphlet in question—a member of your profession, by the way—*tells the truth.* Knowing as I do from remarks that you have let fall that you are *largely a vegetarian,* I feel that under these circumstances to ask you to continue your visits would be not only wrong and *tactless* on my part, but *painful to yourself.*—Yours very truly,

EDITHA BARING-RAYNE

Nov. 4

XII

Mrs. Baring-Rayne to Dr. Tunks

(By hand)

MY DEAR DOCTOR,—I have been a very *impulsive and masterful* woman, but all that is over My heart to-day is *like a little child's,* that knows its *true friends.* Do let us forget this terrible week of misunderstanding and cross purposes. I shall expect you to-morrow morning at half-past

eleven, just as in the *old days.* Imaginative
sympathy is so rare.—Yours sincerely,

EDITHA BARING-RAYNE

P.S.—How odd is this occasional reappearance
of old *forgotten* characteristics! You know how
grey, how *sad,* how *humble,* my life is. Yet
suddenly there breaks out this mood of imperi-
ousness, which years ago at school earned me the
nickname of Boey (short for Boadicea). Where
has it been slumbering all this time? These are
among the mysteries.   E. B.-R.

Nov. 4

IX

The Loin of Pork   ∽   ∽   ∽   ∽

I

*Mrs. Chillingham Bull, of " The Cheviots," Little
Wickling, to Mr. Henry Ings, Butcher, of Little
Wickling*

(By hand)

Mrs. Chillingham Bull finding that her
friendly verbal message by her butler to Mr.
Ings concerning the nuisance caused by his
persistent killing of pigs at the time when she
and her household are at family prayers has had
no effect, now informs him that she intends to
take measures to stop the obnoxious practice.

Sept. 28

II

Mr. Henry Ings to Mrs. Chillingham Bull

(By hand)

MRS. CHILLINGHAM BULL, DEAR MADAM,—It is
my wish to kill pigs as quietly as possible, not

only to cause as little nuisance as I can, but also out of regard to my own and Mrs. Ings's feelings, both of us being sensitive too. The pig which was killed this morning at the time you name in your favour of even date was specially ordered by Sir Cloudesley Scrubbs, and could not be kept back owing to its being market day at Boxton and my killer having to be there.—I am, yours obediently, HENRY INGS

Sept. 28

III

Mrs. Chillingham Bull to Sir Cloudesley Scrubbs

(By hand)

DEAR SIR CLOUDESLEY,—I am sorry to trouble you, but you must put the blame upon my desire to suppress a growing nuisance in our otherwise peaceful village. Ings, the butcher, has contracted the disagreeable habit of killing his pigs between 8.30 and 9, the very time at which we have family prayers, and you cannot conceive how discordant and heartrending are the screams that reach our ears across the lawn at that time. Perks remonstrated with him some time ago, and we thought the matter over; but this morning it broke out again with renewed violence, and on my sending a peremptory note Ings says that

the pig was killed at that hour by your instructions. I shall be glad to hear from you that you
repudiate the responsibility.—Yours sincerely,

ADELA CHILLINGHAM BULL

Sept. 28

IV

Sir Cloudesley Scrubbs to Mrs. Chillingham Bull

(*By hand*)

DEAR MRS. CHILLINGHAM BULL,—It is quite true
that I ordered the pig, as we are expecting friends
who are partial to pork. But I specified no time
for its demise, least of all that half-hour in which
you perform your devotions. Ings, who is the
most civil of men, surely must mean that he
understood I was in a hurry, and therefore
killed the pig directly the post came in.—Believe
me, dear Mrs. Chillingham Bull, yours very
truly, VINCENT CLOUDESLEY SCRUBBS

Sept. 28

V

Mrs. Chillingham Bull to Mr. Ings

(*By hand*)

Mrs. Chillingham Bull having made inquiries
of Sir Cloudesley Scrubbs finds that Mr. Ings was

quite mistaken in thinking there was any need for the killing of the pig to occur when it did, and after what has happened she intends to remove her custom to a Boxton butcher as a mark of her displeasure.

Sept. 28

VI

Mr. Ings to Mrs. Chillingham Bull

(*By hand*)

Mr. Ings presents his compliments to Mrs. Chillingham Bull, and begs to enclose his account of £18, 5s. 6½d., immediate payment of which would oblige. He also wishes to give notice that the next times he catches any of Mrs. Chillingham Bull's fowls in his garden (notice of same having previously been given, and a stoppage of the nuisance promised) he intends to wring its neck.

Sept. 28

VII

Mrs. Chillingham Bull to Sir Cloudesley Scrubbs

(*By hand*)

Dear Sir Cloudesley,—I hasten to send you the enclosed offensive missive from Ings, in response to one from me saying that I could not deal with him any more. I think that you will see the matter in the same light that I do. In such cases neighbours must stand by each other for mutual protection and the harmony of life.—Yours sincerely,

ADELA CHILLINGHAM BULL

Sept. 28

VIII

Sir Cloudesley Scrubbs to Mrs. Chillingham Bull

(*By hand*)

DEAR MRS. CHILLINGHAM BULL,—With every desire in the world to oblige you I do not see my way, as you seem to suggest, to cease to deal with Ings. For one thing we like the quality of his meat ; for another—and you must pardon my frankness—I cannot consider that he has shown anything more objectionable than an independent spirit. You say nothing about the fowls, which he seems to look upon as a grievance at any rate not more imaginary than the pig-killing.—Believe me, dear Mrs. Chillingham Bull, yours very truly,

VINCENT CLOUDESLEY SCRUBBS

Sept. 28

Life's Little Difficulties

Mrs. Chillingham Bull to Sir Cloudesley Scrubbs

(*By hand*)

DEAR SIR CLOUDESLEY,—I am sincerely pained at the view which you take. I cannot see what can come of village life if, as I said before, we do not stand by each other. Ings has been most rude to me, and he must be brought to his senses. —Yours truly, ADELA CHILLINGHAM BULL

Sept. 28

X

Mrs. Chillingham Bull to Mr. Blades, Butcher, Boxton

Will Mr. Blades please send to Mrs. Chillingham Bull to-morrow morning a fore-quarter of lamb and a wing-rib of beef?

Sept. 28

Mr. Perks to Mr. Blades

DEAR SIR,—Mrs. Chillingham Bull, of "The Cheviots," Little Wickling, having decided to change her butcher, and having begun to send you orders, I thought it interesting to let you

know that it was by my advice that her choice
fell on you.—Yours truly,   HENRY PERKS

Oct. 1

XII

Mrs. Chillingham Bull to Mr. Blades

Mrs. Chillingham Bull is very dissatisfied both
with the quality of Mr. Blades's meat and the
excessive proportion of bone and suet, to which
her attention has been called by her butler.
Unless an improvement occurs she will have to
change her butcher.

Oct. 5

XIII

Mrs. Chillingham Bull to Mr. Earwaker, Butcher,
Boxton

Will Mr. Earwaker please send to Mrs. Chillingham Bull to-morrow morning a leg of mutton and
a sirloin of beef?

Oct. 10

XIV

Mr. Perks to Mr. Earwaker

DEAR SIR,—Mrs. Chillingham Bull, of "The
Cheviots," Little Wickling, having decided to

N   193

change her butcher, and having begun to send you orders, I thought it interesting to let you know that it was by my advice that the choice fell on you.—Yours truly,   HENRY PERKS

Oct. 12

XV

Mrs. Chillingham Bull to Mr. Earwaker

Mrs. Chillingham Bull is very dissatisfied both with the quality of Mr. Earwaker's meat and the excessive proportion of bone and suet, to which her attention has been drawn by her butler. Unless an improvement occurs she will have to change her butcher.

Oct. 15

XVI

Mrs. Chillingham Bull to the Rev. Dr. Baylham

DEAR RECTOR,—I am sorry you are away from home, because there is a little difficulty in the village which can be settled only by yourself. Mr. Pipes, though his sermons are irreproachable, and he is most kind, has not the needful tact.

To make a long story short, your petted churchwarden Ings, a few weeks ago, was very rude to me and I had to take away our custom. The Boxton butchers are, however, very bad, and on thinking it over I am inclined to pardon Ings, but I am afraid from the attitude which he took up that he may not accept my forgiveness in the spirit in which it is offered; which would, of course, be very unfortunate and wholly inimical to the harmony of village life. I therefore write to ask you if you would write to him.

Perks, who is much distressed about it all, tells me that we shall never have good meat from the other butchers, and he is continually urging me to return to Ings. Will you not, dear Rector, once more prove yourself the Little Wickling mediator?—Your grateful friend,

ADELA CHILLINGHAM BULL

P.S.—I hope you are enjoying Chamounix. I was there with my dear husband in 1885.

Oct. 17

XVII

Dr. Basil Baylham to the Rev. Gregory Pipes

DEAR PIPES,—Our friend at "The Cheviots" seems to have done something to offend poor Ings, with the result that that good man has been abandoned in favour of the Boxton trade. Knowing both as we do, there can be little doubt as to where the fault lies. Mrs. Bull writes to me asking for my mediation, because, although her spirit is willing to continue the fray, the flesh is weak, and recollections of Ings' excellent fillets seem to be crowding appetisingly upon her, as she struggles with the Boxton gristle. I leave the solution to you with perfect confidence.—Yours,

B. B.

Oct. 20

XVIII

Mr. Henry Ings to Mrs. Chillingham Bull

Received with thanks cheque for £18, 5s. 7d.

HENRY INGS

Oct. 22

```
┌──────────┐
│          │
│  Stamp   │
│          │
└──────────┘
```

XIX

Mrs. Chillingham Bull to Mr. Ings

Understanding from her butler that Mr. Ings has recently killed a pig, Mrs. Chillingham Bull would be glad if Mr. Ings would send her a loin of pork.

Oct. 22

X

The Shade of Blue ⌒ ⌒ ⌒ ⌒

Mrs. Vincent Olly to Mrs. Leonard Sprake
(With enclosure)

MY DEAR VERA,—Do be an angel and go off at once to Ell's or Naval's and see if you can match the enclosed shade in velvet. I want the dress for Friday week, and there isn't a minute to lose. It is for Mrs. Ashley Carbonel's At Home, and you know my reasons for wishing to look well there. I want two yards—and blow the expense, as Vinny says. Don't say you are busy or anything, or I shall have to ask Olive Shackle; and Heaven knows I don't want to be beholden to her any more.—Your frantic   M.

Mrs. Leonard Sprake to Mrs. Vincent Olly

DEAREST MILDRED,—I have been everywhere, and it can't be done. I went first to Ell's, then to Naval's, then to Silkands' and Worcester Nicoll's,

and then back to Bond Street to Bedford and
Hanbury's. But all in vain. I saw nothing that
would match. Tell me what to do next. Why
must you have velvet? I am glad you asked *me*
and not the Shackle girl. After your last experience of her "limpetude," as Len calls it, you
should be very shy. How long was it she stayed?
Two months? Some people are beyond any-
thing.—Yours,   VERA

Mrs. Vincent Olly to Mrs. Leonard Sprake

MY DEAR VERA,—I must have velvet. There
is no way out of it; nothing else will do. Try
Licence's, or one of those Kensington places,
Irving and Queens' or Biter's. Only you must go
at once. I would not trouble you only I cannot
trust anyone else's eye. Yours never makes a
mistake. When we meet remind me to tell
you about Mrs. Glendenning and the Scripture
Reader. It is too delicious; but much too long
to write.—Yours in despair,   M.

Mrs. Leonard Sprake to Mrs. Vincent Olly

DEAREST MILDRED,—I have been to all and not
one has it. The nearest thing was at Licence's,
but they had only a pattern. The material itself

is out of stock and cannot be replaced. I even
tried the wilds of Oxford Street, but all in vain
too. You really must give up the idea of
matching, or try silk. The great joke here is
that at Lady Bassett's last week Canon Coss
found a glass eye in the spinach and cut his poor
mouth horribly. It turns out to have been the
new cook's. Len says there ought to be insur-
ance against such things. If it had been the
Canon's eye and the cook's mouth, there would
be, he says.—Yours,   VERA

Mrs. Vincent Olly to Mrs. Leonard Sprake
(Telegram)

Try Daw's.

Mrs. Leonard Sprake to Mrs. Vincent Olly
(Telegram)

Daw's no good. Do have silk.

Mrs. Vincent Olly to Mrs. Leonard Sprake
(Telegram)

Silk useless. Try Orange's.

Mrs. Leonard Sprake to Mrs. Vincent Olly
(With enclosure)

MY DEAR MILDRED,—I tried Orange's without
avail. I should have gone there sooner, but

knew it would be useless. I now return the
pattern with many regrets. I would have still
made one or two other efforts, but I must go
down to Chislehurst to-morrow to see mother, and
after that it will be too late. I still think you
would have been wiser to try some other material
less difficult to match than velvet. — Yours
with regret, VERA

Mrs. Vincent Olly to Mrs. Leonard Sprake

DEAR VERA,—I think you are very selfish and in-
considerate. Your visit to your mother cannot be so
fearfully important, and I seem to remember other
occasions when she had to stand over for lots of
more attractive engagements. Still, you must, of
course, do what you want to do. I am sending
the pattern to Olive Shackle, who, in spite of her
faults, is, at any rate, zealous and true.—Yours
disappointedly and utterly tired out, M.

Miss Olive Shackle to Mrs. Vincent Olly

MY SWEET MILDRED,—I am sending you the
velvet by special messenger; which is a luxury to
which I am sure you will not mind my treating
myself. I got it at once at Ell's, from my own
special counter-man there. He had put it on

one side for another old customer, but made an exception for me. How I should love to see you in your beautiful dress throwing everyone else at Mrs. Ashley Carbonel's into the shade! I was to have been with the Rutters at Church Stretton for the week-end, but poor dear Mrs. Rutter has just written to say that her sister is dangerously ill at Woodhall Spa with something that may very likely develop into peritonitis, and she has had to put off all her guests.—Yours ever,

OLIVE SHACKLE

Miss Olive Shackle to Mrs. Vincent Olly
(Telegram)

Will come with pleasure.

The Smithsons, the Parkinsons, and Col. Home-Hopkins ⌒ ⌒ ⌒

I

Miss Daisy Hopping to a lifelong school friend
(Extract)

THE news is that mother is going to give another No. 1 dinner party, the first for three years. We are to have waiters from London instead of poor old Smart, the greengrocer, who breathes down your back, and two special *entrées*, and the champagne that grandpapa left us instead of what Dick always calls the Tête Montée brand for local consumption. And the county people are asked this time—no Smithsons and Parkinsons and Col. Home-Hopkins, and the other regular old stodgers who go to all the parties within a radius of six miles. It is all because Uncle and Aunt Mordaunt are coming from India, and he has just got a C.S.I.

The Smithsons, Etc.

II

Messrs. Patti and Casserole to Mrs. Montgomery Hopping

MADAM,—In reply to your esteemed favour of the 22nd we would suggest *quenelles de volaille aux champignons* as one *entrée* and *ris de veau à l'Armandine* as the other. The two waiters will come to you by the 3.5 from Euston.—We are, Madam, yours faithfully,

PATTI AND CASSEROLE

III

Miss Daisy Hopping to the same lifelong school friend. (Extract)

Mother is in her best temper, as all the guests she has asked have accepted. Lena and I are not to come down to dinner, because there won't be room, but we are to go in afterwards, and mother is giving us new dresses. Mine is [*thirty lines omitted.*] So you see it's an ill wind that blows nobody any good. Uncle Mordaunt will talk about Stonehenge all the time, but they all say they are so charmed to be going to meet him.

Life's Little Difficulties

IV

Mrs. Leonard Hatt to Mrs. Montgomery Hopping

DEAR MRS. HOPPING,—I am so very sorry to have to tell you that we shall not be able to dine with you on the 5th after all, as my husband is ill with a chill. You will, I know, be glad to hear that his temperature is now nearly normal, after a very anxious time, but the doctor forbids all thought of going out of doors for at least ten days. I am exceedingly sorry, as we were so looking forward to the evening at your pretty house and to seeing dear Sir Mordaunt again.—I am, yours sincerely,

MILDRED HATT

V

Lady Durdham to the Hon. Mrs. Willie Ross

DEAR NANNY,—We reached town yesterday, after a delightful cruise, and now we want to see you and Willie more than anything, so come up on the 5th, Thursday, and we will go somewhere, and have supper, and talk it all over. If you have an engagement, break it.—Yours,

BEE

The Smithsons, Etc.

VI

The Hon. Mrs. Willie Ross to Mrs. Montgomery Hopping

DEAR MRS. HOPPING,—It is very distressing to me to have to decline an invitation after accepting it, but I have just discovered that we have an engagement for the 5th which cannot be put off. I am so very sorry, and I promise I will never be so careless again—if you ever give me another chance! Believe me, dear Mrs. Hopping, yours **very** truly,

ANNETTE ROSS

VII

Canon Bath to Mrs. Montgomery Hopping

MY DEAR MRS. HOPPING,—I very deeply regret to have to write as I must; but we are all servants and at the mercy of our masters, and the Bishop has just signified his intention of visiting Widdesdon on the day of your charming party, and has asked me to be his host.

To so good a churchwoman as yourself I need not say more, except that I am deeply concerned to have to break faith with you and to miss a congenial antiquarian gossip with

Sir Mordaunt.—Believe me, dear Mrs. Hopping, yours sincerely, OLIVER BATH

VIII

Mrs. Vansittart to Mrs. Montgomery Hopping

DEAR MRS. HOPPING,—I have put off writing till the last moment, hoping that the necessity might pass, but I am now forced to say that I shall not be able to dine with you on the 5th. Poor Arthur was brought home on Saturday, from mixed hockey, so badly bruised and injured that he has been in bed ever since and requires constant attention. I am sure that you (who also are a mother) will understand that I should not like to leave him in this state even for an evening ; and so I hasten to let you know.—Yours sincerely, KATE VANSITTART

P.S.—You will please tell Sir Mordaunt and Lady Hopping that I am deeply grieved not to meet them.

IX

Mrs. Montgomery Hopping to Messrs. Patti and Casserole. (Telegram)

Mrs. Montgomery Hopping will not require either the *entrées* or the waiters for the 5th.

The Smithsons, Etc.

X

Miss Daisy Hopping to the same lifelong school friend. (*Extract*)

This house isn't fit to live in. Everyone who was invited has backed out, except old General Stores, who says he put off going to the South of France on purpose. Mother never thought he would come at all. If it weren't for him, mother (who is more like a whirlwind than anything I ever experienced) says she would have no party at all; but now she must go on with it, especially as she told Uncle Mordaunt. And so it means the Smithsons and the Parkinsons and Col. Home-Hopkins after all. The worst of it is we are not to have new dresses.

XI

Mrs. Parkinson to Mrs. Montgomery Hopping

DEAR MRS. MONTGOMERY HOPPING,—It will give Mr. Parkinson and myself such very great pleasure to dine with you on the 5th to meet your distinguished brother-in-law. A dinner party at your house is always such an event, and in our remote neighbourhood, where excitements are so few, short notice perhaps adds to the delight.—Believe me, yours sincerely,

MILDRED PARKINSON

Life's Little Difficulties

Col. Home-Hopkins to Mrs. Montgomery Hopping

MY DEAR LADY,—Your word is always law,
and you may count on me to be on your hospit-
able doorstep at the stroke of eight. Would
that you had said seven, that an hour of happiness were added! I beg you not to apologise for
what you call short notice. No notice should be
too short to a soldier.—I am, dear Lady, yours to
command, EDGAR HOME-HOPKINS

Mrs. Smithson to Mrs. Montgomery Hopping

MY DEAR MRS. HOPPING,—It would give Mr.
Smithson and myself much pleasure to accept
your kind invitation were it not that we are a
little in bondage to a visitor, a niece of my
husband's, such a very nice girl, who is staying
with us before taking up a position at Cannes as
a companion to a very interesting old lady, the
widow of Commander Muncaster, who, you may
remember, died a few weeks ago. As we do not
quite like to leave Madeline alone all the evening, I wondered if I might bring her with me.
She is a very nice girl, and quite the best pupil
at the Guildhall School of Music last year.

Perhaps you would like her to bring some music with her. I know it is often a help. But of course, dear Mrs. Hopping, you will say at once if it is inconvenient or likely to put your table out, and then we can perhaps get Miss Moberly to come in for the evening and bring her knitting, and keep Madeline company, as I should not like to refuse your very kind invitation. The Doctor was saying only the other day how long it was since we had the pleasure of dining with you. As for short notice, I hope you won't mention it. It is so difficult often to give long notice, as I know only too well.—Yours very truly,

MARTHA SMITHSON

P.S.—I find I have not said how glad we shall be to see Sir Mordaunt and Lady Hopping.

XIV

Mrs. Montgomery Hopping to Mrs. Smart

To MRS. SMART,—I am glad your husband can come for Thursday evening. I am counting on him to be here at five to help with the silver, and I shall want some mushrooms if you can get them, some French beans, and two heads of celery. E. MONTGOMERY HOPPING

XII

"White Pinings"   ∾   ∾   ∾   ∾

I

Miss Vesta Swan to the Thalia and Erato
Press, Ltd.

DEAR SIRS,—I am sending you by registered post the MS. of a volume of poems, entitled *White Pinings,* in the hope that you will like them sufficiently to undertake their publication. The poems are entirely original, and have never before (with one exception) been printed.   It was once my intention to print them from time to time in the better class weekly papers, but after a while that idea was abandoned.   The exception is the rondeau called " Coral Toes," which appeared in the *Baby's Friend,* but there would be no difficulty about copyright, I am sure.—Yours truly,   VESTA SWAN

"White Pinings"

II

The Thalia and Erato Press to Miss Vesta Swan

Dear Madam,—Our Reader reports that he has read *White Pinings* with much interest, and that in his opinion the book is in every way worthy of publication. Poetry, however, as you perhaps are not unaware, is no longer read as it used to be. This apathy is the result, some think, of the interest in motors, but according to others is due to the fashion of Bridge. Be it as it may, no great sale can be expected for such a book, and our Reader therefore suggests that you should combine with us in this enterprise. Of course if the book is successful your outlay would come back to you multiplied many times. We calculate that a first edition of *White Pinings* would cost £100, and we suggest that each of us contributes £50.

Awaiting your reply, we are, dear Madam, yours faithfully,

The Thalia and Erato Press
per A. B. C.

III

Miss Vesta Swan to the Thalia and Erato Press

Dear Sirs,—I am glad to know that your Reader thinks so highly of my book. Would it

Life's Little Difficulties

be indiscreet to ask his name?—there are two or three points concerning the poems which I should like to put to him.

I am aware that the ordinary run of poetry is not profitable, but there are shining examples of success. I have just been reading the Life of the late Lord Tennyson, who seems to have been quite wealthy, although he wrote comparatively little ; and I gather that the Brownings also were well-to-do. One of my friends considers my style not unlike a blend of both Robert and E. B., although (being a woman) naturally more like the latter. I understand also that both Mr. Swinburne and Mr. Alfred Austin are quite comfortably off. So that there are exceptions.

I should say also that *W. P.* is not, as you think, my first book. I published in 1896, through a firm at Winchester, a little collection called *Heart Beats,* a copy of which was sent to Her late Majesty Queen Victoria.

None the less, as I believe in my work and wish others to have the opportunity of being cheered by it, I will pay the £50. Please put the book in hand at once, as I want it to come out with the April buds.—Yours truly,

VESTA SWAN

"White Pinings"

IV

The Thalia and Erato Press to Miss Vesta Swan
(Extract)

We enclose a contract form, which please sign and return to us with cheque. Any letter intended for our Reader will be at once forwarded to him.

V

Miss Vesta Swan to the Reader of her MS.

DEAR SIR,—I should very much like to have your opinion of the "Lines written at midnight after hearing Miss Clara Butt sing 'The Lost Chord.'" Do you think the faulty grammar in line 4 of stanza 2—"loud" the adjective, for "loudly" the adverb—is permissible? I have already spent some time in polishing this poem, but I have so high an opinion of your judgment that I am ready to begin again if you say I should. And do you think the title should be merely *White Pinings* or that it should have the sub-heading — "Sighs of a Priestess of Modernity"? One of my friends, a young journalist, favours the latter very warmly.

I might add that I have a very kind letter from the secretary of Sir Thomas Lipton, who

Life's Little Difficulties

read the poems in MS., praising them in no
measured terms. Do you think it would do the
book good if we were to print this letter in fac-
simile at the beginning?—I am, yours truly,

VESTA SWAN

[Several letters omitted]

XVI

*Miss Vesta Swan to the Thalia and Erato Press
(Telegram)*

Stop printing. Serious misprint, page 41.
"Heave on coal" should be "Heaven our goal."

XVII

*The Thalia and Erato Press to Miss Vesta Swan
(Telegram)*

Too late. Error unimportant.

[Several letters omitted]

XXIII.

*Miss Vesta Swan to the Thalia and Erato Press
(Extract)*

. . . And will you please be sure to send a
copy with the author's compliments to Mr.

" White Pinings "

Andrew Lang, as I hear he is so much interested in new poets?

[From a vast correspondence the following six letters have been selected]

XXXI

Miss Vesta Swan to the Thalia and Erato Press (Extract)

. . . My friends tell me that they have great difficulty in buying *White Pinings*. A letter this morning says that there is not a bookseller in Blackburn who has heard of it.

XLV

Miss Vesta Swan to the Thalia and Erato Press

DEAR SIRS,—Several persons have told me lately that they have looked in vain in the literary papers, ever since *White Pinings* was published, for any advertisement of it, and they have found none. Many of the books of the day are, I notice, advertised very freely, with, I have no doubt, good results—Mr. Hall Caine's last novel, for example. Curiously enough, one of my poems (" An Evening Reverie," page 76), contains very much the same moral as his new book.

Could you not intimate that fact to the public in some way? Please send me twelve more copies.—Yours truly, VESTA SWAN

LIV

Miss Vesta Swan to the Thalia and Erato Press

DEAR SIRS,—In the report in the papers this morning of the Bishop of London's address on the reconcilement of the Letter and the Spirit, there is a most curious anticipation of a statement of mine in the poem, "Let us ponder awhile," on page 132 of *White Pinings*. I think that the enclosed paragraph mentioning the coincidence might be sent to the *Athenæum*. I am told that all the other papers would then copy it.—Yours truly, VESTA SWAN

LIX

Miss Vesta Swan to the Thalia and Erato Press
(Extract)

A friend of mine got out of the train and asked at all the bookstalls between London and Manchester for *W. P.*, and not one had it. Is not this a scandal? Something ought to be done to raise the tone of railway reading. Please send me six more copies.

" White Pinings "

LXVIII

Miss Vesta Swan to the Thalia and Erato Press
(Extract)

I am told that a few years ago a volume of
poems was advertised by sandwichmen in London
streets. Could not *White Pinings* be made known
in this way?

XC

The Thalia and Erato Press to Miss Vesta Swan

Dear Madam,—We have much pleasure in
enclosing the first review of your poems that has
reached us. Doubtless now that a start has been
made, many more will follow.—Yours faithfully,

THE THALIA AND ERATO PRESS
per A. B. C.

[1 Encl.]

From the *Scots Reader*

One of the most amusing misprints that we can recollect
occurs in *White Pinings* (Thalia and Erato Press), by Vesta
Swan, which otherwise is not noteworthy. The poetess
undoubtedly wrote :

"Watch the progress of the soul
Struggling aye to heaven our goal; '

but the waggish printer has made her say,

"Struggling aye to heave on coal."

217

XIII

The Christmas Decorations ✍ ✍

I

*The Rev. Lawrence Lidbetter to his curate, the Rev.
Arthur Starling*

DEAR STARLING,—I am sorry to appear to be
running away at this busy season, but a sudden
call to London on business leaves me no alterna-
tive. I shall be back on Christmas Eve for
certain, perhaps before. You must keep an eye
on the decorations, and see that none of our
helpers get out of hand. I have serious doubts
as to Miss Green.—Yours,   L. L.

II

Mrs. Clibborn to the Rev. Lawrence Lidbetter

DEAR RECTOR,—I think we have got over
the difficulty which we were talking of — Mr.

The Christmas Decorations

Lulham's red hair and the discord it would make with the crimson decorations. Maggie and Popsy and I have been working like slaves, and have put up a beautiful and effectual screen of evergreen which completely obliterates the keyboard and organist. I think you will be delighted. Mr. Starling approves most cordially.— Yours sincerely, MARY CLIBBORN

III

Miss Pitt to the Rev. Lawrence Lidbetter

MY DEAR MR. LIDBETTER,—We are all so sorry you have been called away, a strong guiding hand being never more needed. You will remember that it was arranged that I should have sole charge of the memorial window to Colonel Soper —we settled it just outside the Post Office on the morning that poor Blades was kicked by the Doctor's pony. Well, Miss Lockie now says that Colonel Soper's window belongs to her, and she makes it impossible for me to do anything. I must implore you to write to her putting it right, or the decorations will be ruined. Mr. Starling is kind, but quite useless.—Yours sincerely, VIRGINIA PITT

Life's Little Difficulties

IV

Miss Lockie to the Rev. Lawrence Lidbetter

MY DEAR MR. LIDBETTER,—I am sorry to have to trouble you in your enforced rest, but the interests of the church must not be neglected, and you ought to know that Miss Pitt not only insists that the decoration of Colonel Soper's window was entrusted to her, but prevents me carrying it out. If you recollect, it was during tea at Mrs. Millstone's that it was arranged that I should be responsible for this window. A telegram to Miss Pitt would put the matter right at once. Dear Mr. Starling is always so nice, but he does so lack firmness.—Yours sincerely,

MABEL LOCKIE

V

Mrs. St. John to the Rev. Lawrence Lidbetter

DEAR RECTOR,—I wish you would let Miss Green have a line about the decoration of the pulpit. It is no use any of us saying anything to her since she went to the Slade School and acquired artistic notions, but a word from you would work wonders. What we all feel is that the pulpit should be bright and gay, with some cheerful texts on it, a suitable setting for you

The Christmas Decorations

and your helpful Christmas sermon, but Miss
Green's idea is to drape it entirely in black
muslin and purple, like a lying in state. One
can do wonders with a little cotton-wool and
a few yards of Turkey twill, but she will not
understand this. How with all her *nouveau art*
ideas she got permission to decorate the pulpit
at all I cannot think, but there it is, and the
sooner she is stopped the better. Poor Mr.
Starling drops all the hints he can, but she dis-
regards them all.—Yours sincerely,

CHARLOTTE ST. JOHN

VI

Miss Olive Green to the Rev. Lawrence Lidbetter

DEAR MR. LIDBETTER,—I am sure you will like
the pulpit. I am giving it the most careful
thought, and there is every promise of a scheme
of austere beauty, grave and solemn and yet just
touched with a note of happier fulfilment. For
the most part you will find the decorations quite
conventional — holly and evergreens, the old
terrible cotton-wool snow on crimson background.
But I am certain that you will experience a thrill
of satisfied surprise when your eyes alight upon
the simple gravity of the pulpit's drapery and its

flowing sensuous lines. It is so kind of you to give me this opportunity to realise some of my artistic self. Poor Mr. Starling, who is entirely Victorian in his views of art, has been talking to me about gay colours, but my work is done for *you* and the few who can *understand.*—Yours sincerely,

OLIVE GREEN

VII

Mrs. Millstone to the Rev. Lawrence Lidbetter

DEAR RECTOR,—Just a line to tell you of a delightful device I have hit upon for the decorations. Cotton-wool, of course, makes excellent snow, and rice is sometimes used, on gum, to suggest winter too. But I have discovered that the most perfect illusion of a white rime can be obtained by wetting the leaves and then sprinkling flour on them. I am going to get all the others to let me finish off everything like that on Christmas Eve (like varnishing-day at the Academy, my husband says), when it will be all fresh for Sunday. Mr. Starling, who is proving himself such a dear, is delighted with the scheme. I hope you are well in that dreadful foggy city.—Yours sincerely, ADA MILLSTONE

The Christmas Decorations

*Mrs. Hobbs, charwoman, to the Rev. Lawrence
Lidbetter*

HONOURED SIR,—I am writing to you because
Hobbs and me dispare of getting any justice from
the so called ladies who have been turning the
holy church of St. Michael and all Angels into a
Covent Garden market. To sweep up holly and
other green stuff I don't mind, because I have
heard you say year after year that we should all
do our best at Christmas to help each other. I
always hold that charity and kindness are more
than rubys, but when it comes to flour I say no.
If you would believe it, Mrs. Millstone is first
watering the holly and the lorrel to make it wet,
and then sprinkling flour on it to look like hore
frost, and the mess is something dreadful, all over the
cushions and carpet. To sweep up ordinery dust I
don't mind, more particulerly as it is my paid work
and bounden duty; but unless it is made worth
my while Hobbs says I must say no. We draw the
line at sweeping up dough. Mr. Starling is very
kind, but as Hobbs says you are the founting
head.—Awaiting a reply, I am, your humble
servant, MARTHA HOBBS

Life's Little Difficulties

IX

Mrs. Vansittart to the Rev. Lawrence Lidbetter

DEAR RECTOR,—If I am late with the north windows you must understand that it is not my fault, but Pedder's. He has suddenly and most mysteriously adopted an attitude of hostility to his employers (quite in the way one has heard of gardeners doing), and nothing will induce him to cut me any evergreens, which he says he cannot spare. The result is that poor Horace and Mr. Starling have to go out with lanterns after Pedder has left the garden, and cut what they can and convey it to the church by stealth. I think we shall manage fairly well, but thought you had better know in case the result is not equal to your anticipation.—Yours sincerely,

GRACE VANSITTART

X

Mr. Lulham, organist to the Rev. Lawrence Lidbetter

DEAR SIR,—I shall be glad to have a line from you authorising me to insist upon the removal of a large screen of evergreens which Mrs. Clibborn and her daughters have erected by the organ. There seems to be an idea that the organ is unsightly, although we have had no complaints hitherto, and the effect of this barrier will be to interfere very seriously with the choral part of the service. Mr. Starling sympathises with me, but has not taken any steps.—Believe me, yours faithfully, WALTER LULHAM

XI

The Rev. Lawrence Lidbetter to Mrs. Lidbetter

MY DEAREST HARRIET,—I am having, as I expected, an awful time with the decorations, and I send you a batch of letters and leave the situation to you. Miss Pitt had better keep the Soper window. Give the Lockie girl one of the autograph copies of my *Narrow Path,* with a reference underneath my name to the chapter on self-sacrifice, and tell her how sorry I am that there has been a misunderstanding. Mrs. Hobbs must have an extra half-a-crown, and the flouring must be discreetly discouraged—on the ground of waste of food material. Assure Lulham that there shall be no barrier, and then tell Mrs. Clibborn that the organist has been given a pledge that nothing should intervene between his music and the congregation. I am dining with the Lawsons to-night, and we go afterwards to the *Tempest,* I think.—Your devoted L.

XIV

The Prize Competition ～ ～ ～

I

Miss Bristowe to her niece, Miss Grace Bristowe

My DEAR GRACIE,—Your Aunt Sophie and I
have been thinking so much of late about your
brave resolve to earn a little money for yourself
and be independent of your dear father, who has
burdens enough on his purse, Heaven knows!
We have not heard what you have decided to do,
but have great doubts as to the lasting lucrative-
ness of poker-work, unless done on a very large
scale. And bookbinding, we understand, needs
a long and rather expensive apprenticeship.
Sweet-pea growing, I read somewhere recently,
can be profitable, but that needs not only knowledge but land, and I doubt if your father could
spare you that; and I believe all the glebe is let.

The Prize Competition

Poor man, he will soon need all the rent the glebe brings in if these terrible Radicals have their own way much longer, with their dreadful views about the Church. But what I wanted to tell you was that your aunt, when at a garden party at the Hall yesterday, met a very attractive girl who had already received three guineas in prizes from the *Westminster Gazette,* and is quite confident of making much more. I doubt if you ever see the *Westminster Gazette,* which is certainly not your dear father's colour at all, but it is in other ways quite a nice paper, and really tries to be fair, I think, even if it fails. We see it whenever your uncle comes here, as he always brings it with him. It seems that every Saturday there is a prize competition, with quite good prizes, for literary people, and you were always so clever with your pen. Your aunt says that the one for next week is quite easy—to write a poem of four lines, the first two lines of which end with the words " editor " and " coastguard." The prize is a guinea. Surely you could do that. I will write for a *Westminster Gazette* and send it to you as soon as it comes, with all the particulars.—With love, I am your affectionate

AUNT META

Life's Little Difficulties

II

Miss Grace Bristowe to her aunt, Miss Bristowe

DEAR AUNT META,—How very good of you—
just when I was getting so desperate, too! Of
course I will try—in fact, I have tried already,
but it is not as easy as you think, because there
are so few rhymes to either of the words. Jack
is going to try to get me a cheap copy of a
rhyming dictionary when he goes to town to-
morrow, and I am writing to Uncle Basil to help
me too. Mr. Rainey-Spong is also interesting
himself in it. As he nearly won the Newdigate
and is just bringing out a volume of poetry he
ought to be very useful. We have been having
some ripping tennis this summer.—Much love.
Your loving   GRACIE

III

*Miss Grace Bristowe to her uncle, Basil Heriot, All
Souls' College, Oxford*

MY DEAR UNCLE BASIL,—You are so very
clever, will you help me with a piece of literary
work that I have on hand? I am trying to write
a poem the third line of which must rhyme to
"editor" and the fourth line to "coastguard."
If I do it better than anyone else I shall earn a

guinea, and that is a good deal in these hard times, especially as I want a new driver, and a brassie too. Please write by return of post if you can.—Your loving niece,   GRACE

IV

Basil Heriot to his niece, Grace Bristowe

MY DEAR NIECE,—I fear you have applied to the wrong source, and even if I had any of the mastery of *bouts rimés* with which you are kind enough to credit me, I could not waste any time on such frivolity just now, since all my strength is needed for the completion of the tenth volume of my commentary, and even this letter to you is making sad inroads on the day's routine. I gather from your hurried note that you are competing for some newspaper prize. If you must do such things, I wish you would make an effort to win one of the *Westminster's* guerdons offered for skill in transliterating from the English into Greek. That would be worth doing; but possibly you, with your unfortunate addiction to manly pursuits, are of a different opinion. I wish you would try to be more like your aunt Frideswide, who had written an essay on the *Chanson de Roland* before she was your age and still knows nothing of golf. If ever I can help you in a more serious and worthy difficulty, I shall be glad to make the time ; but before you propound your queries I hope you will be quite sure in your mind that it is I, and I only, who can answer them.—Your affectionate uncle,

BASIL HERIOT

v

Miss Grace Bristowe to her aunt, Miss Bristowe

DEAR AUNT META,—I am not having such an easy time as you expected, and I am beginning to believe in the saying that nothing good is ever done except by hard work. Jack could not get a rhyming dictionary second-hand, and it seemed absurd to spend much on a new one, and the stupid boy hadn't the sense just to turn to those two words in the shop. Uncle Basil, too, was not very helpful. He seems to think that light poetry is hardly worth writing in English at all. As for poor Mr. Rainey-Spong, I happened to mention to father that we were composing a poem in collaboration, and he was furious, and said he did not pay curates for that, and made him visit all kinds of old frumps as a punishment. But I think it will be all right.—Your loving   GRACIE

The Prize Competition

VI

The Rev. Athol Rainey-Spong to Miss Grace Bristowe

Dear Miss Gracie,—I am sending you by Gibbings's boy the fruits of my industry. I wish it could have been more worthy, but I have had an unexpected number of small duties to perform during the past two days.—Yours most sincerely,

A. R.-S.

VII

Miss Grace Bristowe to her aunt, Miss Bristowe

Dear Aunt Meta,—Here it is. Will you please send it in for me, so as to save time? — Your loving niece, Gracie

P.S.—I have already spent half the money on a perfectly adorable puppy—an Aberdeen, quite pure.

VIII

Miss Bristowe to her niece, Miss Grace Bristowe

My very dear Gracie,—I have such sad news for you. The *Westminster Gazette*, which was delayed in the post, has only just come, and I find, to my great disappointment, that there were certain very restricting and, I think, very unfair

Life's Little Difficulties

conditions to that competition. The rules say that neither "creditor" nor "postcard" may be used; and this, I fear, disqualifies your really very excellent poem, which therefore I return. I am so very sorry to have raised your hopes so groundlessly.—Your affectionate   AUNT META

P.S.—I hope you will be able to induce the people to take back the dear little doggie.

IX

The Rev. Athol Rainey-Spong to Messrs. Peter & Co., publishers

DEAR SIRS,—I enclose one more trifle which I should like printed at the end of the book, in the section entitled *Leviore plectro*.

IMPROMPTU

Written at the request of a young lady who supplied the author with the terminal words of the first two lines, and challenged him to complete the quatrain.

> Station is naught. This man's a brilliant editor,
>   And that a simple, plain, unlettered coastguard;
> Yet this one's life's made sad by many a creditor,
>   While that will beam at but a picture postcard.

Believe me, yours faithfully,
ATHOL RAINEY-SPONG

XV

The Cricket Club Concert ✍ ✍ ✍

I

The Rev. Cæsar Dear to Lady Bird

DEAR LADY BIRD, — It will give so much pleasure in the village if you could see your way to carry out a promise which you very kindly made in the summer, and be the moving spirit in the concert which is to be held on the 19th for the Cricket Club. With the many well-known artistes whom you expressed yourself able to induce to perform, the concert cannot but be an unqualified success, and the new roller assured to us.

I might say that the names of Miss Ellaline Terriss and Miss Gertie Millar, whom you felt confident of getting, when placed before the Cricket Club Committee elicited the warmest enthusiasm. So also did that of Mr. Lewis Waller. — Believe me, dear Lady Bird, yours sincerely,

CÆSAR DEAR

Life's Little Difficulties

II

Lady Bird to the Rev. Cæsar Dear

DEAR RECTOR,—I am sorry that engagements keep me in town, as I should have liked to have talked this concert over with you. I will certainly manage it; but I have a feeling—mere instinct, perhaps, rather than reason, but I always trust my instinct implicitly, and have never known it fail me: indeed, all my troubles have come from want of faith in it—that to get London performers would be a mistake. After all, this is a village concert, and the rustics will feel much more at home if the performers are their own people. Will you therefore send me a few names of singers in the neighbourhood to whom I can write? You will be glad to hear that I have prevailed on Sir Julian to tell some stories of Big Game shooting in Nigeria, and my cousin Captain Ide has promised to imitate Mr. Beerbohm Tree. My own contribution will be a share in a little French duologue.—Yours sincerely, MILLIE BIRD

III

Lady Bird to Mr. Hall-Hall

Lady Bird having undertaken, at the request of Dr. Dear, to get up the concert on the 17th,

234

she would be enchanted to learn that Mr. Hall-Hall would be willing to give one of his delightful recitations. Mr. Hall-Hall will be glad to hear that Sir Julian has promised to deliver a short address on his experiences with Big Game in Nigeria.

IV

Mr. Hall-Hall to Lady Bird

Mr. Hall-Hall presents his compliments to Lady Bird and will be very glad to assist in the concert on the 17th. He does not, however, recite, as Lady Bird seems to think, but sings bass.

V

Lady Bird to Miss Effie Plumber

Lady Bird presents her compliments to Miss Effie Plumber, and would be very glad if she would sing at the Cricket Club Concert on the 17th. Lady Bird recently heard a very attractive song called " Hyacinth," which she would recommend to Miss Plumber's notice. Lady Bird herself intends to take part in a short French duologue, and Sir Julian will give the audience the benefit of his Big Game experiences in Nigeria.

Life's Little Difficulties

VI

Miss Effie Plumber to Lady Bird

Miss Effie Plumber presents her compliments to Lady Bird, and begs to say that she will be pleased to sing at the Cricket Club Concert on the 17th. Miss Effie Plumber thanks Lady Bird for her suggestion, but she is in the habit of singing "The Holy City" and "Jerusalem" on these occasions, with, for an encore, "Daddy," and she cannot see any reason for departing from custom.

VII

The Rev. Cæsar Dear to Lady Bird

DEAR LADY BIRD,—Chancing to meet Miss Plumber this morning, I find that she is under the impression that she is to sing for us on the 17th. I hasten to correct this misapprehension, if it is also yours, because the date is the 19th.—I am, dear Lady Bird, yours sincerely,

CÆSAR DEAR

VIII

Lady Bird to the Rev. Cæsar Dear

DEAR RECTOR,—Owing to the very unfortunate way in which you made the figure 9 in your first letter about the concert, I took it for a 7, and have asked everyone for the 17th. Will you therefore change the date to that night?—Yours sincerely, MILLIE BIRD

IX

The Rev. Cæsar Dear to Lady Bird

MY DEAR LADY BIRD,—I regret exceedingly the ambiguity in the numeral. My writing is usually considered so clear. I regret also that the alteration of the date to the 17th is impossible, for several reasons. I have no doubt, however, that you will be able to get most of those who are helping us to come on the 19th, and to find among your great circle of friends and acquaintance others to take the place of the one or two that cannot. I should like to have a complete list of names as soon as possible.—Believe me, dear Lady Bird, yours sincerely,

CÆSAR DEAR

X

Lady Bird to Mr. Hall-Hall

Lady Bird presents her compliments to Mr. Hall-Hall, and regrets to say that, owing to a mistake of the Rector's, the date of the concert was given in her letter as the 17th instead of the 19th. She trusts that the change of evening will make no difference to Mr. Hall-Hall, and that he will still favour the company with one of his charming recitations. Did Lady Bird say in her previous letter that Sir Julian was intending to relate some of his experiences with Big Game?

XI

Lady Bird to the Rev. Cæsar Dear

DEAR RECTOR,—I am very sorry that you will not alter the date. This luckless piece of illegible writing of yours may ruin the whole evening. As my uncle the Archbishop used to say, "Great events often have the smallest beginnings." But now that the date is the 19th for certain, it must not be changed, and we must do what we can. Perhaps the most unfortunate thing is that, on a little capricious impulse, I decided after all that a slight leaven of the real thing might be good, and asked Mr. Hayden Coffin and Miss Isabel Jay for the 17th, and both promised, saying that that night was the only one that was free to them for months and months. This is truly the irony of fate. At present all I can count on is Sir Julian's Big Game stories, which promise to be very interesting, especially as he is taking lessons in elocution; Captain Ide's imitations of Mr.

Beerbohm Tree ; my own share in a little French
duologue ; and a few local efforts, including one
of your friend Mr. Hall-Hall's recitations (not
" Ostler Joe," I hope !).—Yours sincerely,

MILLIE BIRD

XII

Telegram from the Rev. Cæsar Dear to Lady Bird

Am altering date to 17th to secure Coffin
and Jay.   DEAR

XIII

Telegram from Lady Bird to the Rev. Cæsar Dear

Do not alter date. Have just heard both Coffin
and Jay uncertain. No reliance on artistic temperament.   BIRD

XIV

Mr. Hall-Hall to Lady Bird

Mr. Hall-Hall presents his compliments to
Lady Bird, and regrets that he will be unable to
assist in the concert on the 19th by reason of an
old engagement. Mr. Hall-Hall begs again to
assure Lady Bird that he does not recite, but
sings bass.

XV

Lady Bird to the Rev. Cæsar Dear

MY DEAR RECTOR,—I am exceedingly sorry,
but the responsibility of this concert has worn

Life's Little Difficulties

me to such an extent that Sir Julian insists on
our leaving at once for the Riviera. Ever since
the discovery of that unfortunate slip of yours in
the date, I have felt the strain. I am one of those
who cannot take things lightly. I am either all
fire or quite cold. I have been all fire for your
concert and its dear charitable object, and the
result is that I am worn out, consumed. Wreck
though that I am, I would persevere with it to
the end if Sir Julian would allow it; but he is a
rock. I therefore enclose all the correspondence
on the subject, which will show you how the case
stands and make it very easy for you to complete the arrangements. All the hard work is
done.—Believe me, with all good wishes, yours
sincerely,   MILLIE BIRD

P.S.—Sir Julian is having his Big Game
reminiscences type-written for you to read to
the audience. They are most thrilling. I have
instructed Grant to send down the lion-skin
hearthrug for the evening. It should be hung
over a chair so that the two bullet-holes show.
There might be a lighted candle behind it with
advantage

Printed by MORRISON & GIBB LIMITED, *Edinburgh*